ISLAMIC HERITAGE OF GOA

THE HISTORY YOU WEREN'T TOLD
Adil Shahi Mosques of Goa

By

TINUSHA PEREIRA

© 2025 Tinusha Pereira
All rights reserved.

No part of this publication may be reproduced, stored in a retrieval system, or transmitted in any form or by any means, electronic, mechanical, photocopying, recording, or otherwise without the prior written permission of the publisher, except for brief quotations used in critical reviews, scholarly works or other publications that provide clear credit to the author and this work.

First edition: 2025

ISBN: 978-1-7641764-1-5

Cover design and layout by Tinusha Pereira

This is a work of non-fiction. All photographs, illustrations and textual content are either original, used with permission, or sourced under fair use or public domain provisions where applicable. Every effort has been made to trace copyright holders; the publisher will be glad to rectify any omissions in future editions.

For permissions or inquiries, contact:
tinushapereirabooks@gmail.com

Published in Melbourne, Australia.

This book is dedicated to my mama,
Melba Malaika Pereira,
your constant love and faith in me made this book possible.
Thank you for accompanying me to the mosques and helping me with the measured drawings.
I miss you a lot!

Ceiling at the Great Mosque of Isfahan, Iran
Photo by Hossein Monzavizadeh

Table of Contents

Acknowledgments vi

Author's Note vii

List of Figures ix

Introduction 2

Chapter 1: From Kadambas to Adil Shahs to the Portuguese Rule 6

Chapter 2: What is a Mosque? Its Functions and Types Worldwide 10

Chapter 3: Safavid Dynasty: History, Art, Architecture, Religion and Sufism 20

Chapter 4: The Deccan and The Adil Shahs 30

Chapter 5: The Adil Shahs: Connections, Architecture, Trade and Religious Tolerance 50

Chapter 6: Mosques in Goa: Safa Masjid History, Features, Drawings 62

Chapter 7: Mosques in Goa: Surla Masjid History, Features, Drawings 76

Chapter 8: The Forgotten Inheritance: The Adil Shahs and Us 89

Endnotes 103

Bibliography 108

About the Author 111

Acknowledgments

There are so many people I want to thank for this book, I hardly know where to begin.

To all the teachers, mentors and professors who guided me through my thesis in 2009, thank you for your wisdom, encouragement and belief in me.

Thank you to the Archaeological Survey of India, Goa Circle in 2009, and the Directorate of Archives and Archaeology for generously providing valuable information, and to the ASI Dharwad Circle in 2009 for taking the time to show me around and share their insights on the Adil Shahi mosques in Bijapur.

To my dada, Mario, and uncle Ilio, thank you for taking time off to drive me all the way to Bijapur so I could pursue this study.

Thank you to my cousin Narissa, for introducing me to CorelDRAW back in 2011. Your support made those early steps possible.

To my sisters, Tanushka and Tinaika, thank you for always cheering me on! To Tinaika, thank you for accompanying me to the ASI office in Goa last year, and for spending hours with me in the library as I traced the threads of the past.

I also want to thank my mama for her constant support during my research. I only wish she could see the final outcome, this book, and know just how much her belief in me made it possible.

And to my husband, William, thank you for being my biggest cheerleader! You kept encouraging me to finish and publish this book. I'm grateful for your support during our mosque visits last year, and for being my dedicated photographer through it all. I couldn't have done this without you.

To my children, Malaika, Mace and Mitchell. Thank you for your hugs, and your pep talks. Especially Malaika and Mace, who always said, "Mama, you can do this!" You were right. And I did.

Finally, to everyone else who supported me in big and small ways. Your kindness made all the difference. With all my heart, thank you.

Author's Note

The fact that you're reading this, thank you. Truly. I'm grateful that you've taken the time to explore this book, which has been a long time coming.

This project originated as a university thesis in 2009. What sparked it was a simple question: Do we have Islamic heritage in Goa?

I grew up with a sense that Goa was different from the rest of India, being more empathetic, more open and accepting, and that sense shaped how I saw our communities. For my thesis, I wanted to design a structure that reflected this spirit of unity between faiths: Hindus, Muslims and Christians living side by side.

That's when I realized how little I actually know about Goa's Islamic heritage.

So, I began researching about these mosques we heard so little about? Who built them, and why? What were the stories behind them, the people, the rulers, the dynasties? That journey led me to the Adil Shahs.

I had not heard of these Mosques before starting my research. It wasn't something we were taught in school, and it never came up during my five years of architectural studies. It struck me how absent this history was from our books and classrooms, as though it had been silently erased.

This book is a tribute to that often overlooked Adil Shah dynasty and Goa's Muslim Heritage, to their contributions to art, architecture and the cultural fabric of Goa. In many ways, it is also a tribute to how their presence still subtly shapes who we are today, even if we don't always realize it.

This is both a professional and a deeply personal journey for me. I hope this book opens a small window into a part of our heritage that deserves to be seen, studied and preserved.

Above all, this book is my invitation to visit these sites with interest and care and to include them in the way we speak about Goa.

Architectural detail at Cresting of Gol Gumbaz, Bijapur
Photo bt Akash.D

List of Figures:

Fig 1:	Varca Beach, Goa	1
Fig 2:	Basilica of Bom Jesus, Goa	2
Fig 3:	Fontainhas, Goa	3
Fig 4:	Adil Shah Palace / Old Secretariate building, Goa	4
Fig 5:	Tambdi Surla Mahadev Temple Goa	5
Fig 6:	The Ablution fountain of a mosque in Istanbul	9
Fig 7:	Different functions of a Mosque	10
Fig 8:	The Great Mosque of Kairouan, Tunisia	11
Fig 9:	Seyyed Mosque, Isfahan, Iran	11
Fig 10:	Hypostyle Hall Layout	12
Fig 11:	Bi-Axial Four-Iwan Layout	12
Fig 12:	Jama Masjid, Delhi	13
Fig 13:	Hagia Sophia, Istanbul	13
Fig 14:	Triple Domes & Courtyard Layout	14
Fig 15:	Central Dome Layout	14
Fig 16:	Detached Pavilions Layout	14
Fig 17:	Central Pyramidal Roof Layout	14
Fig 18:	Hypostyle Hall using Mud Bricks Layout	14
Fig 19:	Great Mosque of Xi'an, China	15
Fig 20:	Ukuwah Islamiyah Mosque, UI Depok	15
Fig 21:	Great Mosque of Djenné, Mali	16
Fig 22:	Sufi dancer performing on the beach.	17
Fig 23:	Interior Hagia Sophia, Istanbul	18
Fig 24:	Pointed arch, Shah Mosque, Isfahan	19
Fig 25:	View from below of the muqarnas over the entrance Shah Mosque, Isfahan, Iran	21
Fig 26:	Muqarnas st the Chehel Sotoon Palace, Isfahan, Iran	21
Fig 27:	Shah Mosque, Isfahan	22
Fig 28:	Exterior view of the main dome, Shah Mosque, Isfahan, Iran	23
Fig 29:	Interior dome view with polychrome tiles, Shah Mosque, Isfahan, Iran	24
Fig 30:	Entrance to the Shah Mosque, Isfahan, Iran	25
Fig 31:	Jardín de Fin, Kashan, Iran	26

List of Figures:

Fig 32:	Naqsh-e Jahān Square, Isfahan, Iran	26
Fig 33:	Illustration by Cornelis de Bruijn, Dutch painter	27
Fig 34:	Cross-section of a typical qanat	27
Fig 35:	Painting by the French architect, Pascal Coste, visiting Persia in 1841.	28
Fig 36:	Shah Abbasi Caravanserai, Bisotun	29
Fig 37:	Ground floor plan of the Begampur Friday mosque, Delhi	30
Fig 38:	The Quwwat-ul-Islam Mosque, Delhi	30
Fig 39:	Qutub Minar, Delhi	30
Fig 40:	Begampur Masjid, Delhi	31
Fig 41:	Begampur Masjid Iwan, Delhi	31
Fig 42:	The tomb of Alauddin Hasan Bahman Shah, Gulbarga	32
Fig 43:	Jami Masjid in Gulbarga	32
Fig 44:	Slim arches at Jama Masjid, Gulbarga Fort	32
Fig 45:	Squat arches at Jama Masjid, Gulbarga Fort	33
Fig 46:	Schematic map of Bijapur	34
Fig 47:	Illustrated map depicting the political divisions of the Deccan in the 16th century.	34
Fig 48:	Karimuddin Mosque, Bijapur	35
Fig 49:	Illustration of Yusuf Adil Shah	36
Fig 50:	Illustration of Ismail Adil Shah	36
Fig 51:	Illustration of Ibrahim Adil Shah	36
Fig 52:	Inside the Jami Masjid	37
Fig 53:	Jami Masjid, Bijapur	38
Fig 54:	Portrait of Ali Adil Shah I	38
Fig 55:	Gagan Mahal, Bijapur	39
Fig 56:	Sangeet Mahal, Bijapur	40
Fig 57:	Ibrahim Rauza, Bijapur	41
Fig 58:	Jharokha detail, Ibrahim Rauza	41
Fig 59:	Pilaster, Ibrahim Rauza	41
Fig 60:	Procession of Sultan Ibrahim Adil Shah II	42
Fig 61:	Sultan Ibrahim Adil Shah II Venerates a Sufi Saint	42
Fig 62:	Muqarnas seen at Ibrahim Rauza Squinches	43

List of Figures:

Fig 63:	Gol Gumbaz, Bijapur	44
Fig 64:	Whispering Gallery, Gol Gumbaz	44
Fig 65:	Gol Gumbaz tombs	44
Fig 66:	Sultan Mohammed Adil Shah and his prime minister Ikhlas Khan	45
Fig 67:	Asar Mahal, Bijapur	46
Fig 68:	Chihil Sutun Palace, Iran	46
Fig 69:	Ali Adil Shah II	47
Fig 70:	Bara Kaman, Bijapur	47
Fig 71:	Illustration of Sikander Adil Shah	48
Fig 72:	The woodwork inside Asar Mahal, Bijapur	48
Fig 73:	Tomb of Ikhlas Khan, Bijapur	48
Fig 74:	Upli Burj, Bijapur	48
Fig 75:	The House of Bijapur, ca. 1680	49
Fig 76:	Portrait of Shah Ismail I	50
Fig 77:	A structure in Bijapur, commonly identified as a church	51
Fig 78:	Sufi Dancers	52
Fig 79:	Calligraphy at Mihrab at Jami Masjid, Bijapur	53
Fig 80:	Calligraphy at Ibrahim Rauza, Bijapur	53
Fig 81:	Market of Goa	54
Fig 82:	Ibrahim's Old Jami Masjid, Bijapur	55
Fig 83:	Jami Masjid, Bijapur	55
Fig 84:	Ibrahim Rauza Mosque, Bijapur	56
Fig 85:	Bilal mosque, Bijapur	57
Fig 86:	Pointed Arches at Jami Masjid, Bijapur	58
Fig 87:	Mecca Masjid, Bijapur	59
Fig 88:	Mosque in Bijapur	59
Fig 89:	Jahaan Begam Mosque, Bijapur	60
Fig 90:	Safa Masjid, 2009	61
Fig 91:	Site Plan of Safa Masjid	62
Fig 92:	Safa Masjid Site Overview, 2009	63
Fig 93:	Safa masjid Frontal View, 2024	64

List of Figures:

Fig 94:	Longitudinal Site Section of Safa Masjid	65
Fig 95:	Transverse Site Section of Safa Masjid	65
Fig 96:	Architectural Plan of Safa Masjid	66
Fig 97:	Architectural Sections of Safa Masjid	66
Fig 98:	Dargah at Safa Masjid	67
Fig 99:	Dargah of Hazrat Abdul Rehman Qureshi, Safa Masjid	67
Fig 100:	Family Tomb at Safa Masjid	68
Fig 101:	Tomb near Dargah, Safa Masjid	68
Fig 102:	Tombs at Safa Masjid	68
Fig 103:	One of the Laterite Plinths at Safa Masjid	68
Fig 104:	Safa Masjid, Belagavi (Belgaum)	69
Fig 105:	Elevation Drawings of Safa Masjid	70
Fig 106:	Safa masjid Frontal View, 2009	71
Fig 107:	Calligraphy and Pilasters at Ibrahim Rauza	72
Fig 108:	Pilasters on the Mihrab Wall, Safa Masjid	72
Fig 109:	Qibla Wall, Safa Masjid	73
Fig 110:	Safa Masjid in a yellow hue, 2024	74
Fig 111:	Approach to Safa Masjid from the Road, 2024	75
Fig 112:	View of Surla Masjid, 2024	76
Fig 113:	Site Plan of Surla Masjid	77
Fig 114:	Longitudinal Site Section of Surla Masjid	78
Fig 115:	Transverse Site Section of Surla Masjid	78
Fig 116:	View of Surla Masjid, 2024	79
Fig 117:	Surla Masjid Prayer Hall, 2024	80
Fig 118:	Transition Space Before Prayer Hall, Surla Masjid, 2024	80
Fig 119:	Architectural Plan of Surla Masjid	80
Fig 120:	Architectural Sections of Surla Masjid	81
Fig 121:	Elevation Drawings of Surla Masjid	82
Fig 122:	Mihrab of Surla Masjid	83
Fig 123:	Exterior Mihrab projection, Surla Masjid	83
Fig 124:	Mihrab of Safa Masjid	83

List of Figures:

Fig 125:	Exterior Mihrab projection, Safa Masjid	83
Fig 126:	Frontal View of Surla Masjid, 2024	84
Fig 127:	Dargah of Hazrat Pir Saheb, Surla Masjid	84
Fig 128:	Architectural Plan of Safa and Surla Water Tanks	85
Fig 129:	Safa Masjid Water tank 2009	86
Fig 130:	Men are seen performing ablution using the traditional water source, 2009	86
Fig 131:	Women are seen collecting water for household use, 2009	86
Fig 132:	Surla Masjid Water Tank, 2024	87
Fig 133:	Surla Masjid Water Tank from Arches, 2024	88
Fig 134:	Interior view within the arched niches at the Surla water tank	88
Fig 135:	Interpreted Illustration of Safa Masjid with a Dome	89
Fig 136:	Hypothetical Plan of Safa Masjid with a Central Dome	90
Fig 137:	Hypothetical reconstruction of Safa Masjid	90
Fig 138:	Comparative Plans of Safa Masjid, Surla Masjid, and a Typical Bijapur Mosque	91
Fig 139:	Illustration of mosque in Sanquelim	92
Fig 140:	Mosque of the Fortress of Piro, Karwar, Karnataka	93
Fig 141	Illustration of Safa Masjid	94
Fig 142:	View of Safa Masjid, 2024	94
Fig 143:	Chand Bawadi, Bijapur	95
Fig144:	Taj Bawadi, Bijapur	96
Fig 145:	Octagonal tower at Taj Bawadi, Bijapur	97
Fig 146:	Ibrahim Adil Shah II Coppper Coins	97
Fig 147:	Former Adil shah Palace, Panaji, Goa	98
Fig 148:	Adil shah Palace Gate entrance, Old Goa	98
Fig 149:	Safa Masjid, Goa	99
Fig 150:	Looking onto Safa Masjid, Goa	100
Fig 151:	Khandepar Mosque, Ponda, Goa	101
Fig 152:	The Neglected State of the Khandepar mosque, Ponda, Goa	102
Fig 153:	Ruins of the Khandepar Mosque, Ponda, Goa	102

Fig 1- Varca Beach, Goa

Fig 2: Basilica of Bom Jesus, Goa
Photo by vinay442, Pixabay. 2021. [Pixabay License]

INTRODUCTION
Goa beyond the familiar

When people think of Goa, it often brings to mind Instagram-worthy images of sun-kissed beaches lined with coconut palms, winding roads through lush paddy fields, mouth-watering seafood, and that susegad vibe (a Goan philosophy of peaceful, unhurried living) that defines Goan life. Goa is also renowned for its striking monuments: the towering Se Cathedral, the UNESCO-listed Basilica of Bom Jesus, and the elegant temples of Mangueshi and Nageshi in Ponda. These landmarks are more than just popular backdrops for travel blogs. They are living symbols of the rich blend of cultures that shape Goa's unique identity.

Goa was colonised by the Portuguese in 1510 and remained under their rule for over 450 years. Over time, this long period shaped a distinct Indo-Portuguese character that can still be seen in everything from our architecture to our cuisine. But what makes Goa truly special is the way its people live side by side in harmony, whether they are Hindus, Muslims, Catholics, or from other communities. Each community proudly preserves its own traditions while sharing in a collective sense of identity and belonging.

As a child, one of my most vivid memories was our annual visit to Old Goa for the feast of Saint Francis Xavier. The Basilica of Bom Jesus stood tall and majestic, its age-old façade commanding awe and reverence. The crowds were huge, and the air was filled with incense and dust. But the thought of a sausage *pav* (bread) and *Limca* (drink) after church service always gave me something to look forward to. Those experiences, both sensory and spiritual, remain etched in my memory.

Fig 3: Fontainhas, Goa

Fig 4: Adil Shah Palace / Old Secretariate building, Goa
Photo by JoeGoaUk73, Flickr. [CC BY-SA 2.0]

I also remember a 12th-grade school picnic to the ancient Tambdi Surla Mahadev Temple. It was the monsoon season. The air was pleasantly cool and silvered with mist. Nestled in lush greenery, the black basalt temple stood in dignity. It was built during the Kadamba period in the 12th century. Standing before something that had existed for over 900 years felt almost surreal! I found myself wondering about the lives it had witnessed, the prayers it had heard, the silence it had kept through battles and centuries of change. It was both humbling and mesmerizing to be in the presence of something so ancient, so rooted in time, yet still so alive in spirit.

Growing up in Goa, I was always in awe of the churches and temples that defined our spiritual and architectural landscape. But one question lingered in my mind.
Where is the Muslim heritage in Goa? Did Muslims ever rule this land we call home?
For instance, take the majestic Old Secretariat building in Panjim. Many assume it was built by the Portuguese, given its prominent riverside location and colonial past. But what if I told you that this grand mansion, once the residence of the Portuguese viceroy, was not built by the Portuguese at all?
Although the structure has been altered over the centuries, its roots go back to the Adil Shahi period. It was originally built by Yusuf Adil Shah, the 1st Adil Shah ruler of Bijapur. This grand building, once known as the Adil Shah Palace, served as his summer residence.
But who was Yusuf Adil Shah? Why did he build a palace in Goa? And more importantly, what legacy did he and the Adil Shahi dynasty leave behind in this land we call Goa?

This book is a journey to uncover that forgotten chapter. A chapter filled with mosques, Sufi influences, architectural gems, and stories of tolerance and cultural fusion. It is a tribute to a heritage that exists quietly in the background waiting to be rediscovered.

Fig 5: Tambdi Surla Mahadev Temple Goa
Photo by Kbdessai. Wikimedia Commons. [CC BY-SA 4.0]

The Kadambas greatly influenced Goa's heritage, with one of their key contributions being the Tambdi Surla Mahadev Temple, a fine example of Kadamba architecture.

Chapter 1

From Kadambas to Adil Shahs to the Portuguese Rule: Goa's Journey Through Time

Before we explore who Yusuf Adil Shah was and how his reign shaped Goa, it's important to step back and trace Goa's broader historical journey. This brief historical overview provides context for understanding the arrival and influence of the Adil Shahs in Goa. It also highlights how preceding and successive dynasties, and foreign powers helped shape the region's political and cultural landscape, thereby influencing the nature and extent of Adil Shahs rule in Goa.

The Kadamba Dynasty in Goa (10th - 14th Century CE)

From the 3rd to the 14th century CE, Goa experienced the reign of various dynasties, including the Bhojas, Chalukyas, Rashtrakutas, Silharas and Kadambas. Among them, the Kadambas (960 – 1328 CE) emerged as the first major rulers to unify Goa under a single administration. Their reign is often regarded as Goa's first golden age, marked by political stability, cultural growth and thriving trade networks.

The Kadambas established their capital at Gopakapattana (modern-day Goa Velha), which served as a significant port city facilitating maritime trade with the Arab world, the Byzantine Empire and Southeast Asia.[1] This strategic location played a key role in Goa's economic prosperity. Arab traders not only engaged in commerce, but also held high ministerial positions, indicating an early Islamic presence in the region.[2]

A prime architectural legacy from this period is the Tambdi Surla Mahadev Temple, that stands as a reflection of the craftsmanship and cultural heritage of the Kadambas.

Transition to Islamic Rule: Delhi Sultanate and Bahmani Influence (1328 - 1492 CE)

In the 14th century, Goa came under Muslim rule for the first time. It was briefly controlled by the Delhi Sultanate before falling under the influence of the Bahmani Sultanate. This marked the beginning of the Kadamba dynasty's decline, as they eventually lost control to the expanding power of the Bahmanis.

The Delhi Sultanate in Goa (1328-1356 CE)

The Delhi Sultanate, established in 1206 CE, marked one of the earliest Islamic regimes in India. It was founded by Qutb-ud-din Aibak, a former slave of Muhammad Ghori. The Delhi Sultanate expanded under successive dynasties like the Khilji, Tughlaq and Lodi. In 1312 CE, during the reign of Alauddin Khalji, Goa was annexed into the Delhi Sultanate's territory. Later, under Muhammad bin Tughluq, the region remained under the Sultanate control until approximately 1356 CE.

The Bahmani Sultanate in Goa (1356-1378 CE and 1472-1492 CE)

The Bahmani Sultanate, founded in 1347 CE by Hasan Gangu Bahman Shah, emerged as a major power in the Deccan after breaking away from the Delhi Sultanate. According to the historian Firishta, Hasan Gangu was of Afghan birth. The Bahmanis were the first independent Islamic kingdom in the Deccan and were renowned for their patronage of Persian culture, language and literature, which left a lasting impact on the region's administration and cultural life. The Bahmanis ruled Goa from 1356 to 1378 CE. Following a period of Vijayanagar dominance, they regained control of Goa in 1472 CE.

The Vijaynagar Empire in Goa (1378-1472 CE)

Following prolonged conflict between the Bahmani Sultanate and the rising Vijayanagar Empire, Goa came under Vijayanagar rule around 1378 CE, lasting until 1472 CE. Under their administration, Goa became a major trading hub, especially for the import of Arabian horses. However, the Bahmanis eventually reclaimed Goa by 1472 CE.

The Adil Shahi Period in Goa (1498 CE – mid-17th century CE)

In 1492 CE, the Bahmani Kingdom fragmented into five smaller sultanates: Bidar, Berar, Ahmadnagar, Golconda and Bijapur.

It was the Sultan of Bijapur, Yusuf Adil Shah, who seized control of Goa in 1498 CE, establishing his capital at Ela (Old Goa).

Under Yusuf Adil Shah's rule, Goa experienced a period of prosperity and growth. The port city flourished as a vibrant trade hub where Arab horses were imported, and calicoes, muslin, spices and rice were exported. This economic boom marked the beginning of a new era in Goa's commercial history. During his reign, Goa also gained importance as a departure point for pilgrims travelling to Mecca.

Goa was a favoured retreat for the Sultan, and its villages were administered by hereditary headmen known as Gaonkers.[3] The Adil Shah rulers introduced the jagirdari system in Goa. A jagir was a revenue-yielding estate granted typically to families holding high civil or military office, such as the Desais and Sardesais.[4]

Yusuf Adil Shah organised his kingdom's administration by dividing each district into sub-divisions using Persian terms such as pargana, mahal and taluk. In present-day Goa, the term taluka is commonly used, while in Konkani, the traditional term mahal is still in use. These administrative terms introduced during the Adil Shahi period have endured and continue to be part of Goa's administrative vocabulary today.[4a]

Although the Portuguese captured Old Goa in 1510 CE, the Adil Shahs retained control over several Goan talukas for decades. Notably, Bardez and Salcette remained under Adil Shah rule until 1545 CE, when Ibrahim Adil Shah I (1534–1557) ceded these regions to the Portuguese in exchange for political support to secure his throne. The agreement involved the surrender of his brother Prince Abdullah. However the Portuguese did not honour this condition. Instead of surrendering Abdullah, they exiled him to Cannanore to avoid further unrest. Despite this, the Portuguese later breached the terms by bringing Abdullah back to Goa.[5]

While the Portuguese gradually expanded their territory, inland regions such as Ponda, Sanguem, Quepem and Bicholim remained under Adil Shahi control well into the mid-17th century, highlighting the influence of Adil Shahs in Goa's hinterland despite the growing colonial presence.

The Adil Shahi administrative system and cultural presence left a lasting legacy in Goa, reflecting in its language, village organization and the architectural remnants that survive to this day.

The Portuguese Takeover of Goa (1510–1961 CE)

The shift to Portuguese rule in Goa was marked by a mix of diplomatic opportunity, strategic invasion and violent conquest. Initially, the Vijayanagar admiral Timmaya invited the Portuguese to take control of Goa to counter Adil Shahi influence. He informed Afonso de Albuquerque that Goa was vulnerable. Yusuf Adil Shah was away on an expedition, and his governor, Malik Yusuf Gurji, lacked the military strength to defend the city.[6]

Seizing this opportunity, Albuquerque launched an assault and successfully captured Goa with ease in March 1510. However, Yusuf Adil Shah quickly returned and launched a counter-offence. On 17 May 1510, he retook Goa, forcing Albuquerque to retreat to Cochin.

Refusing to concede defeat, Albuquerque regrouped and launched a renewed offence. On 25 November 1510, he successfully recaptured Goa, and to commemorate the victory, the Se Cathedral was erected on the site of a former mosque. As the conquest took place on the feast day of St. Catherine, the cathedral was dedicated in her honour. Tragically, just days later, on 5 December 1510, Yusuf Adil Shah passed away, leaving behind his minor son, Ismail Adil Shah.[7] The regency was handed over to Governor Kamal Khan, but the new administration lacked the strength to challenge the Portuguese.

In retaliation for what was perceived as betrayal by the local Muslim population, Albuquerque ordered a brutal massacre, targeting the city's Muslim inhabitants.[8] The massacre devastated the Muslim community of Goa. This act recorded in Portuguese chronicles and later studies was meant to send a clear message against resistance and to strengthen control over the newly captured city.

Yusuf Adil Shah's Chivalry and Honorable Warfare

A notable aspect of the 1510 siege of Goa was Yusuf Adil Shah's remarkable display of chivalry and ethical conduct in warfare. While the Portuguese fleet was anchored at the mouth of the harbor and suffering from illness and starvation. Yusuf Adil Shah, upon hearing of their plight from deserters, offered provisions. He declared that he wished to defeat his enemies with the sword, not through their starvation. Albuquerque, unwilling to accept aid, staged an illusion of abundance to mislead Yusuf's envoys. Additionally, at Albuquerque's request, Yusuf Adil Shah refused to allow Portuguese deserters to return and weaken their resolve, thus further affirming his adherence to honourable military conduct.[9]

After Yusuf Adil Shah's death, Albuquerque wrote to his son, Ismail Adil Shah, extending offers of friendship and military support, framed as a gesture of respect for his late father. He assured protection for merchants and horses, encouraged diplomatic relations and even promised assistance against Ismail's enemies.[10] However, this outreach was more a strategic move as Albuquerque sought to pacify the young ruler and avert a potential Bijapuri retaliation against the newly captured Goa. Despite this, the Adil Shahis attempted to retake Goa in 1512 but were ultimately unsuccessful.

Between Sword and Treaty: Diplomacy and Discord in Adil Shah-Portuguese Relations

Over the years, the relationship between Bijapur and the Portuguese oscillated between hostility and diplomacy. After the Portuguese captured Goa in 1510, the Adil Shahs made a failed attempt to recapture it in 1512. This initiated a prolonged period of conflict, with renewed hostilities occurring between 1516 and 1545. A peace treaty was eventually concluded in 1546, but tensions and hostilities flared up again in 1570–71 and 1576-77.[11]

Despite these clashes, both powers gradually recognized the strategic importance of cooperation. The Adil Shahs began to rely on the Portuguese for protection and access to maritime trade, while the Portuguese relied heavily on Bijapur for provisions, especially during their conflicts with emerging European rivals such as the British and the Dutch. Over time, an understanding was reached: the Portuguese were allowed to reside peacefully in Goa and govern under their own laws and customs, so long as they did not encroach upon Bijapuri territory.[12] They signed several peace treaties, navigating a relationship marked by both collaboration and underlying tension, which in casual terms could be described as "frenemies."

By the early 17th century, diplomatic relations between the two powers had improved considerably. The reigns of Ibrahim Adil Shah II (1580–1626 CE) and his son Mohammed Adil Shah (1626–1656 CE) saw a period of relative stability and cooperation. The Adil Shahs maintained a permanent ambassador in Goa, while the Portuguese Viceroy sent emissaries to Bijapur only as needed. During his travels in Goa between 1608 and 1610, French navigator François Pyrard de Laval observed the cordial ties between the Portuguese and the Adil Shahi court.[13]

After 1656, Bijapur's attention was increasingly consumed by the growing threat of Mughal expansion under Aurangzeb, which left little room for renewed confrontation with the Portuguese. As a result, from 1656 until the fall of Bijapur in 1686, the relationship between the two powers remained largely peaceful, closing a chapter of fluctuating alliances and enduring rivalries.

The Maratha Presence in Goa (1675-1788)

Chhatrapati Shivaji, the founder of the Maratha empire was crowned at Raigad in 1674.[14] According to historian Prajal Sakhardande, the Maratha foothold in Goa began in 1664, when Shivaji seized Pernem, Bicholim and Sankhli-Sattari from the Adil Shahs. Maratha authority was maintained through local administrators and allied chiefs. In 1675, the Marathas captured Ponda Fort,[15] a strategic victory that enabled Shivaji to expand his influence in the region's interior. Under Maratha rule, the inland talukas witnessed a cultural and religious revival, particularly with the rebuilding of temples like Shantadurga at Kavlem and Mangueshi at Priol.

However, following their defeat at the Third Battle of Panipat in 1761, Maratha influence in Goa began to decline. Between 1763 and 1788,[16] the Portuguese gradually annexed the remaining Maratha-held talukas through a series of treaties, completing what came to be known as the New Conquests.

With the annexation of the New Conquests, the Portuguese finally brought the whole of Goa under their control. They continued to rule the territory until 1961, making it one of the most enduring colonial regimes in the world.

Note: The timeline in this chapter is based on widely accepted scholarly sources, but due to limited records and differing interpretations, dates and events are approximate and may vary slightly across different sources. This note is included in the interest of historical accuracy and transparency.

Fig 6: The Ablution fountain in the courtyard(*sahn*) of a mosque in Istanbul

Chapter 2

What is a Mosque?
Its Functions and Types Worldwide

Before we explore the mosques built by the Adil Shahs in Goa, it's worth pausing to ask what exactly is a mosque? This chapter delves into what defines a mosque and explores its architectural features across different regions of the Islamic world, setting the stage for understanding the Adil Shahi mosques in a broader context.

A mosque is called a *masjid* in Arabic. It is where Muslims come together to pray, reflect and connect as a community. It's not just a place of worship, but also a space where people gather for Friday prayers, celebrate festivals, learn and support one another. In many ways, it's the heart of Islamic life, both spiritually and socially.

Different functions of a Mosque

Mosques vary in design and style depending on the region, historical period, cultural influences and local materials and traditions. However, some essential architectural elements are commonly found in most mosques.

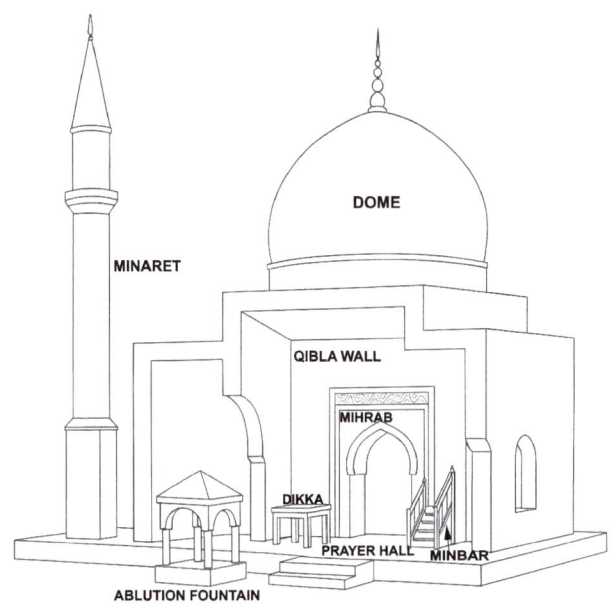

Fig 7: Different functions of a Mosque

Mihrab: It is a beautifully decorated niche in the wall that shows the direction of Mecca, towards which Muslims face during prayer. You'll usually find intricate calligraphy, tilework, or geometric patterns surrounding it. The Mihrab is both functional and symbolic.

Qibla wall: This is the wall that faces Mecca, and the mihrab is located within it. It serves as the physical and spiritual focal point of the mosque.

Minbar (Pulpit): Next to the mihrab, there is usually a raised platform with steps. The minbar is from where the imam (prayer leader) delivers the Friday sermon

Dikka: This raised platform is used in larger mosques where the imam's voice might not carry. It allows the respondents of the mosque to repeat the rituals recited by the imam, transmitting them to a large congregation. Depending on its size and the prevailing climate, the dikka may also be positioned in the courtyard.

Prayer Hall: The prayer hall, or *musalla*, is a large open space where worshippers gather for prayer. It is devoid of furniture as Muslims pray on the floor, and is often covered with carpets.

Domes: Domes are often placed directly above the main prayer hall, symbolising the vaults of heaven and the sky. It also enhances acoustics by amplifying the imam's voice. Its design varies across regions reflecting the artistic traditions of Islamic architecture.

Minarets: These are tall, slender towers usually attached to a mosque or positioned at one of its corners. Traditionally, the muezzin (caller to prayer) would ascend the minaret to deliver the *adhan* (call to prayer) so it could be heard over a wide area. In modern times, this role is typically fulfilled using loudspeakers mounted on the minaret to broadcast the *adhan* to the surrounding community. Minarets vary in design based on cultural influences.

Fig 8: Hypostyle Hall design: The Great Mosque of Kairouan, Tunisia
Photo by Marek Szarejko, Flickr (CC BY-SA 2.0)

Fig 9: Bi-Axial Four Iwan design: Seyyed Mosque, Isfahan, Iran
Photo by Diego Delso, delso.photo (CC BY-SA 4.0)

Ablution Fountain: In Islam, before stepping into prayer, worshippers perform *wudu*. It is a ritual of washing of the hands, mouth, face, arms, head and feet. Traditionally, many mosques featured a central ablution fountain in the courtyard. Today, wudu areas are often located near the mosque entrance and are fitted with rows of low taps and seating.

Sahn (Courtyard): This open courtyard, often found in older or larger mosques, is a place where people gather. It sometimes has a water fountain at the center. It's a space for both purification and community.

Women's Prayer Area: Many mosques have a dedicated space for women, either a separate room or a partitioned section of the prayer hall, ensuring privacy while allowing full participation in congregational worship.

Early mosque layout

Early mosques are believed to have been inspired by the house of Prophet Muhammad in Medina. His residence was a simple mud-brick structure, centered around a rectangular enclosed courtyard with living quarters along one side. On the side facing the qibla, a shaded porch made of palm branches provided shelter for worshippers during prayer. This simple yet functional design laid the groundwork for early mosque architecture, shaping not only the spatial layout but also the communal and spiritual functions of Islamic places of worship for centuries to follow.

The 3 types of mosque

Masjid (General Mosque)

A masjid or general mosque is the most common type of Islamic place of worship. It primarily serves as a space for the five daily prayers, known as *salah*. These mosques can vary in size, from small neighbourhood prayer rooms to larger community spaces. However, their purpose remains the same. They provide a dedicated place for worship, reflection and spiritual connection. Unlike larger congregational mosques, a general masjid typically does not include a minbar (pulpit), as it is not used for delivering the Friday sermon.

Jami Mosque (Congregational Mosque)

A Jami mosque or congregational mosque is usually the largest and most prominent mosque in a region. It is built to accommodate a large congregation, especially during Friday prayers, known as *Jumu'ah,* where the entire community gathers for worship. Beyond the weekly prayers, Jami mosques are often used for major religious events and community gatherings. The Jami mosque features a minbar (pulpit), from which the imam delivers the *khutbah*, or Friday sermon, to the assembled congregation.

Idgah (Eid Prayer Ground)

An Idgah is an open-air prayer ground specifically used for Eid prayers, which takes place twice a year during the Islamic festivals of Eid al-Fitr and Eid al-Adha. Usually found on the outskirts of towns or cities, it's meant to bring the whole community together in one place to pray and celebrate. Unlike a mosque, it isn't used for daily prayers but for festive celebrations and gatherings.

Distinct Styles of Mosque Architecture in Different Regions

Hypostyle Hall and Courtyard (Spain and North Africa): This style features a wide hall filled with rows of columns, often opening out into a spacious courtyard. You'll see it in many mosques across Spain and North Africa.

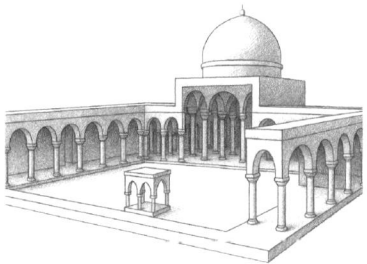

Fig 10: Hypostyle Hall Layout

Bi-Axial Four-Iwan Design (Iran and Central Asia): This style is built around a central courtyard with four large vaulted halls called iwans, one on each side. The layout is perfectly symmetrical and creates a strong sense of balance and order. You'll often see this design in mosques across Iran and Central Asia.

Fig 11: Bi-Axial Four-Iwan Layout

Fig 12: Triple Domes & Courtyard design: Jama *Masjid*, Delhi
Photo by Bikashrd (CC BY-SA 4.0)

Fig 13: Massive Central Dome design: Hagia Sophia, Istanbul
Photo by Arild Vågen (CC BY-SA 3.0)

Triple Domes and Extensive Courtyard (India): Many mosques in Mughal India are instantly recognizable by their three domes, with a larger central dome flanked by two smaller ones, and a spacious open courtyard in front. This style reflects a blend of Persian and local Indian influences.

Fig 14: Triple Domes & Courtyard Layout

Massive Central Dome (Istanbul): Istanbul's mosques are renowned for their massive central domes, symbolizing the grandeur and architectural innovation of the Ottoman Empire.

Fig 15: Central Dome Layout

Detached Pavilions within a Walled Garden (China): Chinese mosques often feature detached pavilions set within a walled garden enclosure, blending Islamic and traditional Chinese architectural elements.

Fig 16: Detached Pavilions Layout

Central Pyramidal Roof Construction (Southeast Asia): In Southeast Asia, mosques commonly employ a central pyramidal roof, portraying the region's adaptation of mosque architecture to local building traditions.

Fig 17: Central Pyramidal Roof Layout

The Hypostyle Hall using mud bricks or rammed earth construction (Sub Saharan West Africa): Mosques often feature hypostyle halls constructed using mud bricks or rammed earth, reflecting local building traditions. They have rectangular layouts with flat roofs supported by columns and reinforced with buttresses. *(wall supports)*

Fig 18: Hypostyle Hall using Mud Bricks Layout

Two sects within Islam: Shia and Sunni

Sunni Muslims make up the majority of the global Muslim population of about 85–90%. They believe that leadership after the Prophet Muhammad should be chosen by the community, which led to Abu Bakr, becoming the first caliph.

Shia Muslims make up about 10–15% of the global Muslim population, with the largest community based in Iran, formerly known as Persia. They believe that leadership after the Prophet Muhammad should have remained within his family, beginning with Ali, the Prophet's cousin and son-in-law.

Fig 19: Detached Pavilions within a garden design: Great Mosque of Xi'an,, China
Photo by chensiyuan (CC BY-SA 4.0)

Fig 20: Central Pyramidal Roof design: Ukuwah Islamiyah Mosque, UI Depok
Photo by BlackKnight (CC BY-SA 3.0 / GFDL)

Fig 21: Hypostyle hall using mud bricks design: Great Mosque of Djenné, Mali
Photo by Ruud Zwart (CC BY-SA 3.0)

The largest branch of Shia Islam is Twelver Shi'ism, which centers on a belief in twelve divinely appointed leaders, known as the Twelve Imams, with Ali as the first. They believe that the twelfth Imam, Imam al-Mahdi, did not die but entered a state of occultation, and will one day return as the promised Mahdi, a messianic figure who will restore justice and peace.

Despite their differences, both Sunnis and Shias deeply revere the Prophet Muhammad and regard the Qur'an as the divine and unaltered word of God.

Sufism

Sufism is the spiritual heart of Islam. It focuses on a deep and personal connection with God. It's about turning inward, seeking the Divine not just in prayer, but in everyday moments, in silence, in poetry, and in love. Sufis often follow a spiritual guide, someone who helps them navigate this inner journey. Through practices like meditation, chanting (*dhikr*) and acts of devotion, they try to cleanse the heart and draw closer to the presence of God. At its core, Sufism is about love, humility and the longing to know God not just through belief, but through direct experience.

Dargahs are shrines built over the graves of Sufi saints and serve as places of devotion, pilgrimage, and communal gatherings. Visitors often come to dargahs to offer prayers, seek blessings, or pay respects to the saint. The tradition of visiting saints' tombs originated in the early centuries of Islam, (between 7th-10th century) especially in Persia, Central Asia and the Middle East, where tombs of pious figures became centres of devotion. As Sufism spread across the Islamic world, this practice followed. Dargahs are known by different names, maqbara in Iran, türbe in Turkey and dargah in South Asia.

Fig 22: Sufi dancer performing on the beach
Photo by Leo Arslan, sourced from Pexels.com, used under the Pexels license. Edited by Author

Fig 23: Interior Hagia Sophia, Istanbul

"The dome of Hagia Sophia in Istanbul, originally a basilica and later a mosque, shows the intertwining of spirituality and architectural innovation. The large dome draws the eye upwards, inviting worshippers to contemplate higher realms."
— *Kagan Keçeci, The Role of Domes in Islamic Architecture, Dok Mimarlık, January 5, 2025*

Fig 24: Pointed arch, Shah Mosque, Isfahan
Photo by Luis Bartolomé Marcos (CC BY-SA 4.0) Edited by Author

Chapter 3

Safavid Dynasty:
History, Religion, Sufism, Art and Architecture

We've seen how the Bahmani Sultanate laid the foundation as the first independent Islamic kingdom in the Deccan. Its court culture, architecture and intellectual life deeply influenced by Persian traditions. At the same time, Persia itself was undergoing a transformation. By the early 16th century, as the Adil Shahs were establishing their rule in Bijapur and Goa, a powerful new dynasty had risen in Persia—the Safavids. They went on to define the largest and most influential Shia state of their time. The cultural and religious ties between Persia and the Deccan were more than mere coincidences, they were connections. In this chapter, we journey to the heart of the Safavid Empire to understand how it shaped not just a nation, but an entire spiritual and architectural legacy that influenced regions far beyond its borders, including the mosques of the Deccan sultanates and Adil shahi Goa

Origins and Rise of the Safavid Empire

The Safavid dynasty was founded by Shah Ismail I in 1501, marking the rise of a powerful empire in Persia (modern-day Iran). The Safavids traced their ancestry to the Safaviyeh Sufi order, a prominent Sufi mystical movement that emerged in the 14th century. Ismail I claimed descent from Sheikh Safi-al-din Ardabili, the founder of this spiritual order, and considered himself the 19th descendant of the seventh Shia Imam in the Twelver Shi'ism tradition.[17] Upon coming to power, the Safavids introduced a defining shift in the region's identity by establishing Twelver Shi'ism as the official state religion, setting Persia apart from its predominantly Sunni neighbours.

Religion and Sufism

The Safavid Empire is best known for making Shia Islam the official religion of their kingdom, a decision that was both spiritual and strategic. By embracing Shi'ism, the Safavids weren't just shaping religious life; they were also uniting their people, setting themselves apart from powerful Sunni rivals, and building stronger ties with the Shia clergy. This bold move helped give Persia a distinct identity, one that still defines Iran today, and it gave the Safavid rulers a deeper sense of political and spiritual legitimacy in the eyes of their followers.

The Safavids didn't just rule with political power, they came from a deeply spiritual background. Their roots lay in the Safaviyeh Sufi order, that played a central role in the establishment of the dynasty, and Sufism had a lasting impact on the cultural and spiritual life of the empire. This connection to Sufism shaped the way they ruled and the way people lived. Sufi teachings were part of daily life, from the royal court to the everyday people. This spiritual foundation gave the empire a distinct character, where faith and governance, mysticism and identity were deeply connected.

Safavid Architecture

The Safavid architectural style was deeply influenced by both the Timurid (14th – early 16th century CE) and Seljuk (11th – 13th century CE) dynasties. From the Timurids, the Safavids adopted key elements such as axial symmetry, monumental double domes and intricate tilework which were a rich blend of Persian, Turkic and early Mughal designs. The Seljuks introduced architectural features such as the four-iwan courtyard plan, a layout that remained central to Iranian mosque architecture.

Building upon these foundations, Safavid mosque architecture evolved into a distinct and celebrated style, marked by the use of large domes, tall minarets, pointed and ogee arches and vibrant ceramic tile façades. While inspired by their predecessors, the Safavids also introduced innovations of their own, enhancing these inherited forms with refined craftsmanship, elaborate ornamentation and a heightened sense of spiritual grandeur that defined the architectural identity of their era.

Architectural Features in Mosques

Arches: The most prominent form was the four-centered arch, also known as the Persian arch, characterized by its broad span and shallow point at the apex. These arches framed monumental iwans, entrance portals and arcaded courtyards in mosques, madrasas and palaces. They are

Fig 25: View from below of the muqarnas over the entrance Shah Mosque, Isfahan, Iran
Photo by Diego Delso (CC BY-SA 4.0)

Fig 26: Muqarnas st the Chehel Sotoon Palace, Isfahan, Iran
Photo by Esin Üstün (CC BY 2.0)

gracefully elongated, creating a sense of openness and balance, and are often adorned with polychrome tilework, calligraphy, and muqarnas vaulting.

Muqarnas: One of the most distinctive decorative features in Safavid mosque architecture is the use of Muqarnas. They are intricate stalactite-like ornamentation that creates a honeycomb or geometric cascading effect. Often placed at the transition points between walls and domes, as well as in niches, squinches and arched doorways, muqarnas serve both aesthetic and structural functions. They soften architectural transitions while adding depth and texture to the space. In Safavid buildings, muqarnas were often richly glazed in vibrant tiles, enhancing the feeling of spiritual elevation and creating an almost celestial quality within the prayer space.

Fig 27: Shah Mosque, Isfahan
Photo by Skot (CC BY-SA 4.0)

Tilework: It reached new heights during the Safavid period, becoming one of the most celebrated elements of Persian architectural decoration. In Isfahan, the Safavid capital, this art form reached its peak. Mosques and madrasas were adorned with stunning blue and turquoise glazed tiles, forming intricate geometric patterns, floral motifs and elegant Arabic calligraphy. These tiles covered walls, domes, minarets and entrance portals, turning the buildings into vibrant expressions of faith and beauty.

Minerats: During the Safavid era, Minarets evolved from their original functional role into more ornamental and symbolic features. Typically placed in pairs flanking the main entrance or large iwans, they were richly decorated with turquoise and cobalt blue tiles, reflecting the colour palette of the domes and façades. They added verticality to the mosque's profile, guiding both the eye and the spirit upward.

Fig 29: Interior dome view with polychrome tiles, Shah Mosque, Isfahan, Iran
Photo by Diego Delso (CC BY-SA 4.0)

Facing Page
Fig 28: Exterior view of the main dome, Shah Mosque, Isfahan, Iran
Photo by Moe.Sasan (CC BY-SA 4.0)

Domes: They were a defining feature of Safavid architecture, both in scale and symbolism. Often rising above prayer halls and central spaces, these monumental domes were meant to inspire awe by drawing the gaze

Fig 30: Entrance to the Shah Mosque, Isfahan, Iran
Photo by Mr. Minoque (CC BY-SA 2.5) Edited by Author

upward, towards the divine and elevate spiritual experience. The double-shell dome inherited from Timurid influences became a signature Safavid innovation, allowing for impressive height and visual lightness. Constructed primarily from fired bricks, the domes were typically covered in glazed blue and turquoise tiles, sometimes accented with golden stars or calligraphy. Inside, they were often intricately decorated with muqarnas, floral patterns or radiating motifs, giving a celestial feel to the interior space. The domes of mosques like the Shah Mosque and Sheikh Lotfollah Mosque in Isfahan remain some of the most iconic and admired in Islamic architecture.

Calligraphy: Calligraphy was a fundamental element of Safavid architecture, serving both decorative and spiritual purposes. It was commonly used to frame arches, domes and iwans, often appearing in the form of epigraphic bands that highlighted key architectural features. The Safavids favored elegant scripts such as thuluth for monumental inscriptions and nastaliq for more fluid, poetic texts. Often integrated with geometric and floral patterns, calligraphy enhanced the visual flow and expressed the religious and cultural identity of the Safavid state.

Inspired by the Charbagh layout, the garden reflects classic Persian design

Fig 31: Jardín de Fin, Kashan, Iran
Photo by Diego Delso (CC BY-SA 4.0)

Fig 32: Naqsh-e Jahān Square. Isfahan, Iran
Photo by Reza Sobhani (CC BY-SA 4.0)

Fig 33: Illustration by Cornelis de Bruijn, Dutch painter, writer and traveller, depicting Chahar Bagh in Isfahan during his visit between 1703–1704. *Public Domain*

Gardens

The Safavids were renowned for their remarkable achievements in garden design and water management. Persian gardens during the Safavid period were designed as earthly reflections of paradise with a strong emphasis on symmetry, harmony and spiritual symbolism. They incorporated the Charbagh layout—a four-part garden design divided by two intersecting water channels, symbolizing the rivers of paradise described in the Qur'an.[18] Beautiful examples of gardens include the Naqsh-e Jahan Square, Chahar Bagh Avenue, Meidan Square of the Great Mosque in Isfahan and the royal gardens of Isfahan.

Water System

Persian cities were planned with organized urban spaces, parks and gardens, all supported by advanced water management systems that served both public and private needs. One of the most remarkable development was the qanat system—an ancient method of channelling water from highland aquifers through underground tunnels to irrigate fields and supply urban settlements. These underground channels protect the water from contamination and evaporation, ensuring a clean and reliable source. The Safavids inherited this rich tradition and further developed it, incorporating qanats, cisterns, reservoirs and public water tanks into city planning.[19] These systems were especially prominent in Isfahan, where water infrastructure became a vital part of both daily life and the aesthetic design of the city.

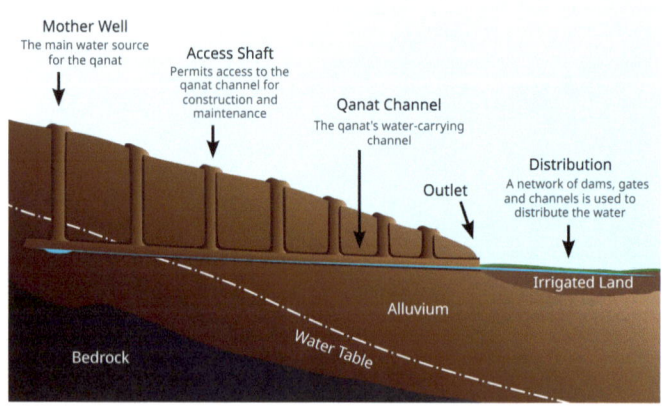

Fig 34: Cross-section of a typical qanat
Illustration by Samuel Bailey (CC BY 3.0)

Fig 35: Painting by the French architect, Pascal Coste, visiting Persia in 1841. The painting shows the main courtyard, with two of the iwans.
Public Domain. Edited by Author

The Safavid Empire played a pivotal role in shaping Iran's religious, cultural and architectural identity. Its official embrace of Shia Islam, close ties to Sufism and advancements in urban planning, gardens and water systems helped define the character of early modern Iran. Architecturally, the Safavids introduced innovations in the use of arches, domes, tilework and the four-iwan mosque plan, creating a distinctive style that blended aesthetic beauty with spiritual meaning. Their contributions not only transformed the skylines of cities like Isfahan but also left a lasting imprint on Islamic architecture beyond Iran's borders. In India, Safavid influence can be seen in Mughal architecture, particularly in the garden char bagh design and decorative elements. More significantly, their architectural style, especially the use of monumental arches and bulbous domes deeply influenced the Deccan Sultanates, including the Adil Shahis of Bijapur, who blended Persian forms with local traditions to create some of the most iconic monuments in South India.

The Safavid Caravanserais

They were a crucial aspect of Persian architecture and urban development during the Safavid dynasty (1501–1736). Caravanserais were roadside inns or rest stops designed to accommodate travellers, merchants and their animals along trade routes, ensuring the safe and efficient movement of goods and people. The Safavid period saw the flourishing of caravanserais as a result of increasing trade, particularly along the Silk Road and Persian trade routes.

The typical layout of a Safavid caravanserai included a central open courtyard usually surrounded by arcaded corridors or rooms on all four sides. The rooms or spaces in the caravanserai were often designed with vaulted ceilings and arched entrances. The corridors provided shelter from the sun and wind and were sometimes designed with an ogee arch or pointed arches, which were typical in Persian architecture during the Safavid period.

Safavid Trade Routes with South India

The Safavid Empire (1501–1736) had significant commercial and diplomatic exchanges with South India, particularly with the Deccan Sultanates and the Mughal-controlled port cities. Persian merchants and traders were active in Indian Ocean trade, and South India was an essential destination for Safavid goods such as silk, carpets, ceramics and horses.

The Safavid Empire maintained vital trade connections with South India through both maritime and overland routes. The Persian Gulf–Arabian Sea route linked Bandar Abbas and Hormuz with key South Indian ports such as Goa, Calicut (Kozhikode), Masulipatnam and Pulicat, facilitating the exchange of silk, carpets, turquoise and ceramics for South Indian spices, textiles, pearls and diamonds. Overland, the Deccan Sultanates (Bijapur, Golconda, Ahmadnagar) shared strong Persian cultural and trade ties, attracting Persian merchants who settled in the region to trade horses, firearms and luxury goods. The Safavids also played a crucial role in supplying warhorses to the Deccan rulers, who relied on them for military campaigns.[20]

Fig 36: Shah Abbasi Caravanserai, Bisotun
Photo by Farzad Menati (CC BY 4.0). Adapted by the author.

Chapter 4
The Deccan and the Adil shahs

Before we delve into the architectural marvels of the Adil Shahi dynasty, it's essential to understand the broader landscape of the Deccan sultanate architecture.

The advent of Muslim rule in India began with the establishment of the Delhi Sultanate in the late 12th century. One of its earliest architectural legacies is the Quwwat-ul-Islam Mosque, constructed in 1193 CE by Qutb-ud-din Aibak. It stands as Delhi's first mosque and a significant example of early Indo-Islamic architecture. It features a rectangular courtyard surrounded by covered passages constructed from intricately carved columns and architectural elements originally part of Hindu and Jain temples.

The Qutub Minar, located within the same complex, was commissioned by Qutb-ud-din Aibak and later completed by his successors. Rising to a height of 73 meters, it was built primarily as a symbol of Islamic victory and supremacy, marking the establishment of Muslim rule in Delhi.

In the 14th century, monumental mosques like the Begampur Masjid further reflected Delhi's growing architectural ambition. The Begampur Friday Mosque, built in 1343 CE in Delhi during the Tughlaq dynasty, follows a traditional hypostyle layout with a central courtyard enclosed by arcades. What sets it apart is the use of four iwans on each side of the courtyard, marking the first known instance of the Persian iwan style being incorporated in India.[22]

Fig 38: The Quwwat-ul-Islam Mosque, Delhi
Photo by Dennis G. Jarvis, India-0357. CC BY-SA 2.0.

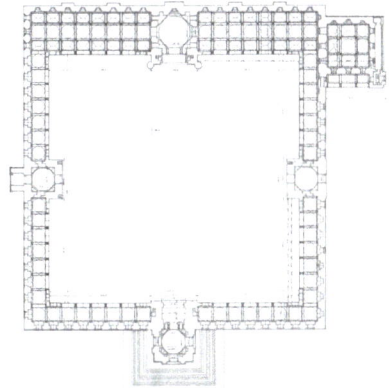

Fig 37: Ground floor plan of the Begampur Friday mosque, Delhi. *Public Domain*
Not to scale

Fig 39: Qutub Minar, Delhi
Photo by Govind K, CC BY-SA 4.0.

Fig 40: Begampur Masjid, Delhi
Photo by Meenakshi madhavan, CC BY 2.0.

When Muhammad bin Tughlaq shifted his capital from Delhi to Daulatabad in the Deccan in 1327 CE and later back to Delhi, numerous skilled artisans migrated to the Deccan region. This migration facilitated the fusion of Persian architectural traditions with Tughlaq architectural styles. The Persian influence became particularly prominent as talented Persian architects and craftsmen designed and executed various structures, significantly enriching the architectural heritage of the Deccan.

Initially, Bahmani architecture closely followed the Tughlaq architectural style, as evidenced by the Tomb of Alauddin Hasan Bahman Shah (1358 CE) located in Gulbarga. The structure exhibits Delhi's characteristic sloping walls, shallow domes and fluted corner turrets.

The Jama Masjid in Gulbarga Fort (1367 CE) represented a significant turning point in Deccan Islamic architecture. It introduced slim and squat arches and prominently featured the Persian dome with a tall drum.[21]

The walls no longer sloped inward, and the domes were bulbous, set upon tall drums, highlighting strong Persian influences.

Fig 43: Jami Masjid in Gulbarga
Photo by Lala Deen Dayal, Public Domain

Photographed in the 1880s, the image captures the prominent dome resting on a drum, a characteristic feature of Persian mosque architecture.

Fig 42: The tomb of Alauddin Hasan Bahman Shah, Gulbarga
Photo from Wikimedia Commons, CC BY-SA 4.0.

Facing Page bottom: Fig 41: Begampur Masjid Iwan, Delhi
Photo by Varun Shiv Kapur, CC BY 2.0.

Fig 44: Slim arches at Jama Masjid, Gulbarga Fort
Photo by Abdul Sohail, CC BY-SA 4.0. (Modified by Author)

Fig 45: Squat arches at Jama Masjid, Gulbarga Fort
Photo by Itsmalay, CC BY-SA 4.0.

Squat and Slim arches at the Jama Masjid in Gulbarga, have finely carved muqarnas decorating the squinches. A distinctive feature of Persian mosque architecture.

Bijapur

In 1294 CE, Alauddin Khalji first captured Bijapur from the Yadavas and annexed it into the Delhi Sultanate. As mentioned earlier, the Bahmani Sultanate later emerged in the Deccan, breaking away from the Delhi Sultanate under the leadership of Alauddin Hasan Bahman Shah. Over time, the Bahmani Sultanate itself fragmented into five smaller successor states — Bidar, Berar, Ahmadnagar, Golconda and Bijapur, each developing its own distinct architectural and cultural identity while maintaining connections to their shared Bahmani heritage.

Bijapur, the capital of the Adil Shahi dynasty, was located on low-lying terrain, surrounded by hills that acted as a natural defense. Yusuf Adil Shah, the dynasty's founder, fortified his capital with a massive citadel, surrounded by circular walls and strengthened with 96 bastions *(projecting parts of a fort wall for defence)* and five principal gates.

Within its walls, he laid the groundwork for the city's growth and development which were later expanded by his successors. The Adil Shahs mainly used locally available basalt stone to build their mosques, tombs, gateways and palaces.

The region received little rainfall, making water conservation essential for the city's survival. To overcome this, the Adil Shahs developed an elaborate system of wells (bawadis) and reservoirs, channelling water from the nearby hills through a network of clay pipes. This system ensured a steady water supply to the city's palaces, mosques, gardens and public spaces.

Over time, the city flourished as a centre of culture and power, known for its grand architecture, vibrant artistic scene and the patronage of poets, scholars and Sufi saints.

In 2014, the Government of Karnataka officially changed the name of the city from Bijapur to Vijayapura. The earliest known reference to the name Vijayapura, meaning 'City of Victory' in Sanskrit, appears in a Western Chalukya inscription dated to the 11th century, discovered within the fort area of Bijapur. The name Bijapur was derived from the name Vijayapura.

However, to maintain consistency and reflect its historical context during the Adil Shahi period, this book will refer to the city as Bijapur throughout.

To truly grasp the legacy of the Adil Shahi dynasty, I embarked on a research trip to the ancient city of Bijapur. Entering Bijapur feels like stepping back into the time of the Adil Shahis, revealing a historical landscape filled with beautiful mosques, ancient tombs, sacred dargahs and majestic palaces.

According to the Archaeological Survey of India (ASI), Bijapur Circle, the city once housed over 300 mosques and 200 dargahs, reflecting its rich architectural and cultural heritage.

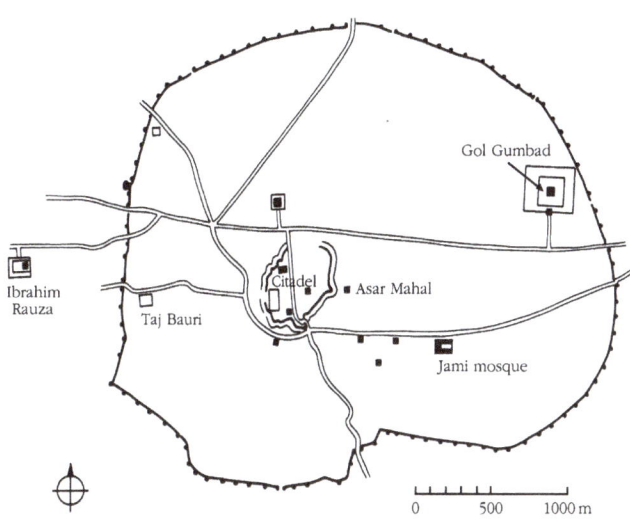

Fig 46: Schematic map of Bijapur
Photo from Wikimedia Commons. Public domain.

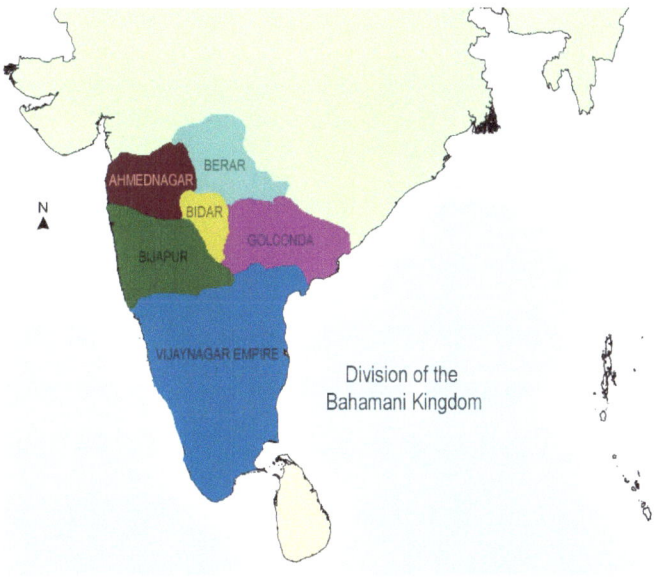

Fig 47: Illustrated map depicting the political divisions of the Deccan in the 16th century.

Fig 48: Karimuddin Mosque, Bijapur

The Karimuddin Mosque, built in 1320, is the earliest known mosque in Bijapur dating to the pre-Adil Shahi period. It was built entirely from reused temple columns and beams, rearranged to form a simple, flat-roofed prayer hall supported by rows of stone pillars.

The Adil Shah Rulers

Each Adil Shah ruler left a lasting mark on the architectural landscape of Bijapur and Goa. Their reigns saw the evolution of mosque architecture, reflecting not only religious devotion but also the personal tastes, political aspirations and cultural engagements of the sultans. As we explore the legacies of these rulers, we will uncover how their visions and influences shaped the monuments that stand the test of time.

1) Yusuf Adil Shah (1489 CE - 1510 CE)

He founded the Adil Shahi dynasty and constructed the citadel in Bijapur. Believed to be the younger son of the Sultan of Constantinople, he escaped death ordered by his sibling by fleeing to Persia. He was sold into slavery to bahmani sultanate's prime minister Mahmud Gawan around 1461, where he ascended to become Governor of Bijapur after Gawan's execution.

In 1489, he declared Bijapur's independence from the Bahmani Kingdom. His reign saw the expansion of his territory to include Goa by 1498 CE. As a devout Shiite, Yusuf Adil Shah was the first Muslim ruler in India to officially propagate Shi'ism, deeply influenced by the contemporaneous rise of the Safavid Dynasty in Persia (1501 CE).[23]

Yusuf Adil Shah was known for his tolerance towards people of different faiths. The Portuguese nicknamed him "Sabaio," The term is believed to be derived from the Castilian word "Sabaio-rios," meaning Sabbath-keepers. This title, initially used in a negative context, reflected the Sultan's acceptance, as he allowed Jews to settle in Old Goa (Ela) and permitted the construction of synagogues. Alternatively, some historical accounts suggest that the title may have originated from his upbringing in the city of Sawa, Persia.[24]

2) Ismail Adil Shah (1510 CE - 1534 CE)

Ismail was around twelve or thirteen years old when he succeeded his father. Kamal Khan, Yusuf Adil Shah's minister was appointed regent and being a Sunni, reinstated Sunni Islam in Bijapur. After reclaiming his rights, Ismail rewarded his loyal supporters, granting Khusro Aqa the title of Asad Khan along with the fort of Belgaum. Strengthening his rule, he continued his father's efforts to establish Shi'ism as the state creed.[25] Ismail Adil Shah actively cultivated ties with Iran and was formally addressed as 'Shah' by Shah Ismail in 1519, thereby asserting Bijapur's status above other Deccani sultanates. Deeply influenced by Iranian culture, he introduced Shia court customs, required his officers to wear the Shia headdress and ordered the Safavid ruler's name to be recited in Friday prayers.[26] He was also a patron of the arts and excelled in painting, music and poetry.

3) Mallu Adil Shah (1534 CE)

He was the older son of Ismail Adil Shah. He wasn't a competent king and within seven months was overthrown by his brother Ibrahim Adil Shah 1.

4) Ibrahim Adil Shah I (1534 CE-1557 CE)

He was a brave ruler, known for fighting on the frontline in many battles. However, his fiery temper and harsh nature were equally notable. He was quick to punish even the smallest of offenses with severe consequences.

He started his reign by implementing major reforms, restoring Sunni Islam and removing many Shia officials appointed by his predecessors. He brought back Deccanis and Abyssinians to key positions, increased Hindu representation in government and made Marathi the official language, replacing Persian.[27]

He is credited with initiating the construction of the Safa Masjid in Goa under the supervision of his governor, Asad Khan. Additionally, he was married to Asad Khan's daughter.

Top Left: Fig 49: Illustration of Yusuf Adil Shah
Bottom Left: Fig 50: Illustration of Ismail Adil Shah
Middle Right: Fig 51: Illustration of Ibrahim Adil Shah

All three illustrations are from The House of Bijapur, ca. 1680. Originally by Kamal Muhammad and Chand Muhammad. Edited by the author. Courtesy of the Metropolitan Museum of Art.

Fig 52: Inside the Jami Masjid
Photo by Mukul Banerjee, (CC BY-SA 3.0)

5) Ali Adil Shah I (1557 CE - 1580 CE)

Upon ascending the throne, he reinstated the Shia faith with the backing of his guardian. He invited followers from Persia and beyond to Bijapur to strengthen his support. Though tensions with the Sunnis nearly led to conflict, he won over the people through his justice and generosity.[28]

He was a warrior king, often depicted in armor and sword in hand. However, his interest in literature and the arts is also notable. Historical records mention his royal library, overseen by a guard, and a workshop of sixty men created manuscripts for his collection. Some of the works were the Aja'ib al-Makhluqat (Wonders of Creation, ca. 1560) and the Nujum al-'Ulum, a guide to astrology and magic.[29]
Historical accounts suggest that he travelled with a vast collection of books during his journeys and military campaigns and invited Portuguese clerics to Bijapur to learn about Christianity.[30]

Fig 53: Jami Masjid, Bijapur

The Jama Masjid of Bijapur, commissioned by Ali Adil Shah I, around 1576 CE, is not only the largest mosque in Bijapur but also one of the most remarkable in the Deccan. The mosque features a vast open courtyard bordered by arcaded halls, a grand dome and an exquisitely ornamented mihrab (prayer niche). One of its most distinctive features is the lotus petal motif encircling the base of the dome. It's an elegant fusion of Persian aesthetics and local Indian design. Despite its grandeur, the mosque was never fully completed.

Fig 54: Portrait of Ali Adil Shah I
Photo from Wikimedia Commons. ca. 1570, Public domain.

Fig 55: Gagan Mahal, Bijapur

He played a key role in the Battle of Talikota in 1565 CE,[31] where the combined forces of the Adil Shahs and other Deccan Sultanates defeated the Vijayanagara Empire and seized its enormous wealth. This victory brought wealth and resources to Bijapur, leading to a period of architectural growth and urban development. During his reign, he built the grand Gagan Mahal and many other structures. His reign also saw major improvements in the city's water supply system, with the construction of numerous tanks, wells and other waterworks to support the growing population.

Gagan Mahal, also known as the "Heavenly Palace," was built in 1561 and it served as a combination of a palace and audience hall. It features a Darbar Hall on the ground floor, with the royal residential quarters situated above. One side of the hall is completely open, allowing spectators unobstructed views into the events taking place within. Gagan Mahal, along with the adjoining palaces, formed the royal centre of Bijapur and was enclosed by a moat and citadel walls.

Fig 56: Sangeet Mahal, Bijapur

6) Ibrahim Adil Shah II (1580 CE -1626 CE)

During his reign, Bijapur flourished as a cultural hub, embracing Hinduism, Sufism, and the formalization of Sunnism as the state religion in 1583.[32]

Ibrahim Adil Shah II sought to bridge divides between Shias and Sunnis, as well as Hindus and Muslims, using music as a unifying force. He was a lover of music and a skilled instrumentalist.

His court attracted artisans, writers and thinkers from across the Islamic world, making Bijapur the leading centre for painting in the Deccan. He was often referred to as 'Jagat Guru,' or 'world teacher.'[33]

Renowned for his patronage of the arts, he built the Sangeet Mahal, a grand palace where musicians from various countries performed and where poets recited their works.

"Standing on the grand platform of the Sangeet Mahal, I imagined the anticipation of the crowds, the vibrant music, the performances and poetic words, all bringing the rich history vividly to life."

Fig 57: Ibrahim Rauza, Bijapur

Ibrahim Rauza is the burial place of Ibrahim Adil shah II and his family members. The complex comprises of a mosque and a tomb, both situated on a raised plinth with a central water tank. The tomb at Ibrahim Rauza features a striking hanging ceiling, composed of precisely fitted stone slabs laid edge to edge, without the use of visible supports.

Ibrahim Rauza reflects the cultural fusion that defined the Adil Shah court. Ibrahim II was known for his deep appreciation of diverse artistic traditions, and his tomb complex represents a blend of Persian, Deccan, Hindu and even Portuguese-Goan influences. The façade of the tomb is adorned with intricate Quranic inscriptions, reminiscent of those found in Safavid Iran.

Fig 58: Jharokha detail, Ibrahim Rauza

Fig 59: Pilaster, Ibrahim Rauza

Fig 60: Procession of Sultan Ibrahim Adil Shah II.
Attributed to a Bikaner painter. ca. 1595, Public domain.

Fig 61: Sultan Ibrahim Adil Shah II Venerates a Sufi Saint
by 'Ali Riza, Bijapur, ca. 1620–30. British Museum. Public

Pilasters, similar to those at Safa Masjid, Goa, and a jarokha feature reflecting local Hindu architectural traditions stand out prominently.

Ibrahim Adil Shah II is credited with composing the Kitab-i Nauras (Book of Nine Essences), which highlights key artistic achievements of the period and uses the concept of nauras as a symbol in state affairs. The book is filled with romantic metaphors, revealing Ibrahim II's blend of religious beliefs, including devotion to Saraswati, the Hindu goddess of music and learning, as well as references to Muslim scholars.[34]

In the above picture, Ibrahim Adil shah II bears around his neck four strings of rudraksha berries, a sign of his increasing devotion to Hinduism.

Ibrahim Adil Shah II was also deeply influenced by Sufism, often embracing its practices and ideals. His court was a hub for Sufi scholars, and he supported the spread of Sufi teachings, blending them with his own policies of religious tolerance and cultural harmony.

Renowned for his amiable and peaceful nature, Ibrahim Adil Shah II maintained harmonious relations with his neighbours and people of diverse faiths, earning a reputation as 'a friend to all foreigners.'[35]

Firishta, the Persian historian, also mentions that Ibrahim Adil Shah II was known for his religious tolerance and diplomatic ties with the Portuguese. His court maintained friendly relations with them, and he skilfully balanced religious and political influences, encouraging trade and strategic alliances.

Fig 62: Muqarnas seen at Ibrahim Rauza Squinches

Fig 63: Gol Gumbaz, Bijapur

Fig 64: Whispering Gallery, Gol Gumbaz -*Photo by Ashwin Kumar Flickr (CC BY-SA 2.0)*

Left: Fig 65 Gol Gumbaz tombs- *Photo by Ashwin Kumar Flickr (CC BY-SA 2.0)*

The main chamber of Gol Gumbaz houses the tombs of Mohammed Adil Shah, his wives and his daughters.

Fig 66: Sultan Mohammed Adil Shah and his prime minister Ikhlas Khan Riding an Elephant.
Photo from Wikimedia Commons. ca. 1645, Public domain.

7) Mohammed Adil Shah (1626 CE-1656 CE)

He was the second son of Ibrahim Adil shah II and assumed the throne at a young age. He inherited the rich and diverse ruling traditions of his father and lead a strong era in Bijapur's history. However, behind the scenes, the true power lay with the ambitious African prime minister, Ikhlas Khan (d. 1656).[36]

Depicted in the above illustration alongside the sultan atop the royal elephant, he symbolized the authority he wielded behind the throne.

Mohammed Adil Shah maintained strong trade relations with the Portuguese, with daily exchanges of goods between Bijapur and Goa.[37]

The mausoleum of Sultan Mohammed Adil Shah, Gol Gumbaz was built in 1656 and has one of the largest domes in the world, measuring 38 meters in internal diameter. This massive, unsupported dome surpasses the size of St. Paul's Cathedral in London (30.8 meters) and closely rivals the domes of St. Peter's Basilica in Vatican City (41.47 meters) and the Pantheon in Rome (43.3 meters). Right above the tombs, it has the circular whispering gallery, an acoustic marvel where even the softest whisper travels across the vast chamber, echoing multiple times. While St. Paul's Cathedral also has a famous Whispering Gallery, Gol Gumbaz's is the largest in the world!

Fig 67: Asar Mahal, Bijapur

The construction of the Asar Mahal is said to include wood, believed to have been imported from Goa, as conveyed through verbal communication with the Archaeological Survey of India (ASI), Bijapur Circle.[38]

Mohammed Adil Shah built the Asar Mahal in 1646 as a "Hall of Justice," similar to the Chihil Sutun palace which was built around the same time in Isfahan, Iran. Both structures feature a tall portico entrance, a reflecting pool and wall fresco paintings reflecting Persian architectural influences.[39] Fresco paintings are also seen at the pavilion at Kumatgi and the Sat-Manzil, Bijapur.[40]

Fig 68: Chihil Sutun Palace, Iran
Photo by Seier+Seier, Flickr, CC BY 2.0

Fig 70: Bara Kaman, Bijapur

Bara Kaman, meaning "Twelve Arches," stands today as a striking reminder of the Adil Shahi dynasty's grand architectural ambitions and the eventual decline of their power.

8) Ali Adil Shah II (1656 CE-1672 CE)

After the death of Mohammed Adil Shah, Bijapur began to weaken by Mughal and Maratha invasions. Ali Adil Shah II ascended the throne of Bijapur in his young adulthood. His reign was marked by constant conflict, particularly against Aurangzeb's expanding Mughal forces and Shivaji's growing Maratha power. Despite efforts to strengthen his rule through diplomacy and military campaigns, Bijapur steadily lost territory and influence. Being a patron of art and architecture, he commissioned the Bara Kaman, envisioned as a grand mausoleum surpassing Gol Gumbaz. However, his premature death at 35 left the structure incomplete, making it the final major architectural achievement of the Adil Shahs.[41]

Fig 69: Ali Adil Shah II
Photo from Wikimedia Commons. ca. 1660, Public domain. Edited by Author

9) Sikander Adil Shah (1672 CE - 1686 CE)

Sikander Adil Shah was the last king that ascended the throne of Bijapur in 1672 at the age of five, following the death of his father. As a minor, his reign was controlled by powerful court nobles, and the kingdom was already weakened from the expanding Mughal Empire under Aurangzeb.

Fig 71: Illustration of Sikander Adil Shah
From The House of Bijapur, ca. 1680. Public Domain. Edited by

The Adil Shahi dynasty ruled Bijapur for nearly 200 years before being absorbed by the Mughal Empire in 1686.

Fig 73: Tomb of Ikhlas Khan, Bijapur

Ikhlas Khan served as the influential Prime Minister of Muhammad Adil Shah, guiding the kingdom's administration and development.

Fig 72: The woodwork inside Asar Mahal, Bijapur.
The construction of the Mahal is said to include wood, believed to have been imported from Goa, as conveyed through verbal communication with the Archaeological Survey of India (ASI), Bijapur Circle.

Fig 74: Upli Burj, Bijapur
This 24-meter-high watchtower was built by the Adil Shahs. Two massive cannons mounted at the top, signify its original defensive purpose in the city's fortifications.

Chapter 5

The Adil shahs:
Connections, Architecture, Trade and Religious Tolerance

After exploring the contributions of each Adil Shah ruler to art and architecture, we now turn to the dynasty's foreign connections and trade relations. These external influences played a significant role in shaping their governance and architectural vision, reflecting a rich blend of cultures, ideas and religious tolerance. We will also examine the distinct architectural styles that emerged in their mosque designs.

Shi'ism and Connection between the Safavid Dynasty and the Adil Shahs of Bijapur.

Shi'ism, also known as Shia Islam, is one of the two main branches of Islam, the other being Sunni Islam. Shia Muslims form a minority of the global Muslim population. Shi'ism emphasizes the importance of justice, resistance to oppression and the spiritual authority of the Prophet's family. These core principles define Shia identity and have historically fuelled movements for social and political change.

Before being sold as a slave and brought to India, Yusuf Adil Shah spent time in Persia, where he was deeply influenced by Shia practices and traditions. These religious and cultural influences were later promoted and expanded by the Safavid dynasty.

As a devoted adherent of Shi'ism, Yusuf Adil Shah played a pivotal role in introducing Shia doctrine in Bijapur, making him the first Muslim ruler in India to officially propagate Shi'ism. This proclamation encouraged even more Iranians to immigrate, and the Adil shahs employed them as soldiers and administrators. Iranian merchants plied the horse trade from the Persian Gulf to Bijapur and Shi'ite notables also achieved high office under Adil Shahi rule.[42]

Being contemporaries, The Adil Shahs sought to align themselves culturally and politically with the Safavid Empire. This religious affiliation helped shape the identity of the Adil Shahi dynasty and influenced the political and cultural development of Bijapur.

Cultural, religious and political ties between the two dynasties led to the promotion of Persian language, art and architecture in Bijapur.

Facing Page: Fig 75: *The House of Bijapur, ca. 1680.*
by Kamal Muhammad and Chand Muhammad. Metropolitan Museum of Art. Edited by the author

The painting portrays the eight Sultans of Bijapur, with Yusuf Adil Shah seated at the centre on the throne, surrounded by his successors.

Fig 76: Portrait of Shah Ismail I, founder of the Safavid Dynasty
Wikipedia, Public Domain

Shah Ismail I, the founder of the Safavid dynasty in Persia, recognized the rule of Ismail Adil Shah in Bijapur, which was a notable gesture of political alignment. This recognition helped establish a stronger bond between the two powers. Additionally, Shah Ismail I sent gifts to Ismail Adil Shah, which was a customary diplomatic practice to affirm their ties and goodwill.[43]

The Adil Shahs sent frequent embassies to the court of Tahmasp I, the second ruler of the Safavid dynasty.[44] These embassies helped in securing political, military and religious alliances between the two dynasties and strengthened their mutual interests.

Fig 77: A structure in Bijapur, commonly identified as a church, believed to have been utilized during the Adil Shahi period.

Jesuits in Bijapur

The Jesuit letters and accounts preserved in the private archives of the Society of Jesus in Europe provide valuable insights into the missions of several priests to the court of the Adil Shahs and the diplomatic relations between Bijapur and Goa. Jesuit letters written in South India to their superiors describe the activities of these missionaries and the interactions between the Bijapur Sultanate and the Portuguese authorities in Goa

According to Jesuit letters in 1561, Ali Adil Shah I requested the Archbishop of Goa, Dom Gaspar de Lea Perura, to send a learned priest to help him understand Christian teachings. In response, the Archbishop sent three clergy members: Jesuit Fr. Gonzalo Rodrigues, Dominican Fr. Antonio Pegado and possibly Fr. Francisco Lopes.[45]

Mohammed Adil Shah employed Jesuit physicians for the treatment of himself and his family, demonstrating his trust in Portuguese doctors.[46]

During Mohammed Adil Shah's reign in 1651, he invited Jesuits to his court, seemingly as part of an effort to recover a valuable diamond that had found its way to Goa and was held by Fr. Gonsalo Martine.

Ibrahim Adil Shah II's court consistently hosted an ambassador from Goa, reflecting his diplomatic skills and friendly disposition, which earned him the title "a friend to all foreigners". He warmly welcomed Jesuits and allowed Portuguese residents to practice their religion under the protection of the ambassador. Several peace treaties were signed between Bijapur and the Portuguese during his reign.

Jesuit missionaries had been active in Bijapur since 1561, when Fr. Gonzalo Rodrigues visited the court of Ali Adil Shah I.[47]

The Jesuits played a key role as intermediaries between the

Fig 78: Sufi Dancers
Photo by Mona Hassan Abo-Abda (CC BY-SA 4.0) Edited by Author

Portuguese and the Adil Shahs, assisting diplomatic communication and helping maintain peace treaties between them. Their presence in Bijapur and other Deccan regions was part of the Portuguese strategy to influence local rulers and strengthen their foothold in India.[48]

The Adil Shahs were also recognized for their religious tolerance, as evidenced by the presence of a structure reportedly used as a church by Jesuits, a fact corroborated by the Archaeological Survey of India (ASI) Bijapur Circle.[49]

Sufis in Bijapur

Early Sufi missionaries arrived in India with the first Muslim armies, gaining popularity among the people and rulers as spiritual and political guides. During the Adil Shahi period, many Sufi saints settled in Bijapur, promoting peace and submission to God through Islamic teachings. The Adil Shahs integrated Sufis into their secular government, with rulers like Ibrahim Adil Shah II following Sufi saints. Some Bijapur Sufis collaborated with the court and received land grants, while others focused on spreading their ideas through literature. They often attracted spiritual descendants and disciples, resulting in clusters of tombs near dargahs. The art, poetry and music of the Deccani courts were highly regarded by the Persians. The Adil Shahs, in turn, warmly welcomed poets, Sufis, artisans, scholars and merchants of Persian origin.[50]

In Bijapur, Sufi saints of every rank formed spiritual lineages and held allegiances as powerful as those of its kings. Their presence is frequently depicted in paintings in the Adil Shahi period.[51]

Fig 79: Calligraphy at Mihrab at Jami Masjid, Bijapur
Photo by Tanya, Public Domain

Calligraphy in Bijapur and Persia

During the late 16th century, calligraphy flourished under the reign of Ibrahim Adil Shah II, whose court attracted a vibrant community of artists, calligraphers and musicians. Persian poetry and Quranic verses were widely incorporated into architecture. The highly esteemed Nasta'liq script, was widely used in Safavid Persia and later adopted by the Deccan Sultanates, especially Bijapur.

Among the notable calligraphers was Khalilullah, a royal scribe who served both Safavid Shah Abbas I and Ibrahim Adil Shah II, earning the prestigious title of "Padishah-i Qalam" (King of the Pen) at the Bijapur court.[52]

Notable examples of calligraphy in Bijapur's monuments include the Ibrahim Rauza, which bears finely carved Persian verses honouring Ibrahim Adil Shah II, featuring poetry and praises for the sultan. The Jama Masjid is another significant example, with beautifully inscribed Persian calligraphy adorning its mihrab.

There are no traces of calligraphy on the surviving mosques in Goa, likely because calligraphy peaked during Ibrahim Adil Shah II's reign in the 1580s to early 17th century, while the existing Goan mosques are believed to predate this period.

Fig 80: Calligraphy at Ibrahim Rauza, Bijapur

Fig 81: Market of Goa print from Jan Huygen van Linschoten's Itinerario
Photo from Wikimedia, Commons, Public Domain

The Market of Goa print from Jan Huygen van Linschoten's Itinerario (1595) offers a vivid glimpse into the bustling trade in Goa on the main street. Trade was restricted to just two hours, from 7 to 9 a.m., making the square crowded and intense.[61] Merchants from various parts of Europe, such as Portugal, Italy and Germany, are seen gathered in groups, negotiating and exchanging goods. Goa's marketplace served as a key link in the Indian Ocean trade, where spices, textiles, gems and exotic goods were actively traded. The presence of foreign traders, enslaved labourers, and elite buyers reflects the complex economy that connected Goa to Africa, Europe and Asia.

Trade in Goa during the Portuguese and the Adil Shahi Period

During the reign of Yusuf Adil Shah, Goa was known for its excellent natural harbor and was an established centre of shipbuilding. The Adil Shahs maintained control over the lucrative horse trade, importing horses from Persia and Arabia, not only for its own cavalry but also for supply to other inland Deccan sultanates. As cavalry played a vital role in asserting military dominance, the control of the horse trade became a strategic asset for the Adil Shahs.[53]

In addition to shipbuilding, the Adil Shahs operated a gunpowder factory in Old Goa.[54] The presence of this facility indicates the dynasty's engagement in military-industrial activity, producing gunpowder locally to support its army and fortifications.

Following the Portuguese conquest of Goa in 1510, the region's trade was absorbed into a wider European colonial maritime network. In 1530, Goa was officially declared the capital of the Portuguese Empire in Asia,[55] becoming a thriving commercial and administrative centre.

Maritime trade in the Indian Ocean was strictly regulated under the Cartaz system, a naval licensing regime imposed by the Portuguese. These cartazas were unique documents that authorized and monitored shipping routes and trade goods. They specified the number of ships the Bijapur Sultanate could send annually to ports in the Persian and Arabian Gulf, and included lists of restricted and permitted imports and exports. The Portuguese also reserved the right to inspect and seize Adil Shahi vessels at will, further asserting their maritime dominance.[56]

Under Portuguese rule, Goa's economy flourished through the export of spices, notably black pepper and cardamom, as well as cotton textiles. A significant portion of the cargoes on homeward-bound ships from Goa consisted of Gujarati goods, particularly cotton cloth.[57] Imports into Goa included gold and silver coins, along with European staples such as wine and olive oil.[58] The Portuguese Crown held a strict monopoly over key commodities, especially spices and horses, regulating their trade closely. Goa also became a centre of Christian missionary activity, influencing not only religion but also trade in books, printing materials and liturgical goods.[59]

The city's strategic importance was not lost on the Adil Shahs. Ibrahim Adil Shah II (1580–1626) and his successor Mohammed Adil Shah (1626–1656) maintained cordial trade relations with the Portuguese and continued daily trade exchanges with Goa. During the Adil Shahi era, Goa saw the export of spices, cotton textiles, diamonds and areca nut, while importing a diverse range of luxury and military items such as precious stones, pearls, Persian silks, brocades, horses, dry fruits and weapons.[60]

Mosques during the Adil shah period

The mosques of Bijapur reflect the growth of architecture and religious life in the city under the Adil Shah rulers. With their support, Bijapur grew into an important Islamic centre. In fact, according to historical sources like Henry Cousens, there were once as many as 1,600 mosques in the city during the reign of Ibrahim Adil Shah II.

Simple Beginnings : The Early Mosques

The earliest mosques built by the Adil Shah rulers in Bijapur reflect the modest beginnings of their kingdom. The structures were functional, less ornamentation and deeply rooted in local Deccan building traditions.
During the reign of Ismail Adil Shah (1510–1534 CE), mosque architecture in Bijapur was in its formative stage. One of the most significant examples from this early period is Yusuf's Old Jami Masjid, built in 1512 CE within the fortified city. Though believed to have been constructed during Ismail Adil Shah's reign, it was commissioned by a Bahmani ruler, Sultan Muhammad Shah. An inscription above the doorframe indicates Bahmani control over Bijapur at the time.[62] This mosque is the oldest dated mosque in the city and is a modest structure built using rubble masonry.[63] The prayer hall has three bays or arches, a feature common in Bijapur mosques. The mosque has a single hemispherical dome surmounted on a tall drum. Its base is surrounded by a ring of vertical foliation that creates the impression of a bud encircled by petals. At the four corners of the mosque are small domed *chhatris* (pavilions) with a decorative base and a simple wooden *chajja* (projected eave) along the structure.[64]

The Introduction of Raised Plinths and the Absence of domes

A major shift in Adil Shahi mosque architecture began with the introduction of raised plinths, which are stone platforms that elevated mosques above ground level, enhancing their presence and significance. The Ibrahimpur Mosque, built in 1526 CE during the later years of Ismail Adil Shah's reign, is the first known example of this style.[65] It marked the beginning of a new architectural approach centered on elevation. Interestingly, the mosque has no dome,[66] which is quite rare for the period. The design is simple and elegant, with a flat-roofed prayer hall and plain arches.
Another example from this period is Ibrahim I's Old Jami Masjid, built in 1551 CE by Ibrahim Adil Shah I. This mosque is particularly interesting because it was built without a dome, with its tall minarets rising from all four corners and one central pillar in the front.

Fig 82: Ibrahim's Old Jami Masjid, Bijapur

Wealth, Power and Persian Influence

The architectural landscape of Bijapur underwent a dramatic transformation after the Battle of Talikota in 1565 CE, during the reign of Ali Adil Shah I. (1558–1580 CE). The Adil Shahs, along with other Deccan Sultanates, defeated the Vijayanagara Empire and plundered its immense wealth. This wealth allowed the Adil Shahs to build larger and grander monuments than ever before.
From this period onward, Persian influence became much more visible in Bijapur's mosques. Persian craftsmen and architectural ideas found their way into the city, blending beautifully with local styles.
The finest example of this new phase is the Jama Masjid of Bijapur, commissioned by Ali Adil Shah I around 1576 CE. This mosque is not only the largest in Bijapur but also one of the most impressive in the Deccan. It has a vast open courtyard surrounded by arcaded halls, a large dome and a richly decorated mihrab (prayer niche). There is a lotus petal design that runs around the base of the dome, a perfect example of how Persian artistic elements were blended with local Indian motifs.

Fig 83: Jami Masjid, Bijapur
Photo by Venkygrams(CC BY-SA 4.0) Edited by Author

Fig 84: Ibrahim Rauza Mosque, Bijapur
Photo by Vivek B Govindaraju (CC BY-SA 4.0) Edited by Author

Above is the image of the mosque at Ibrahim Rauza. It is built on a raised plinth with arches along its base. The mosque reflects the flourishing reign of Ibrahim Adil Shah II, with its onion-shaped dome flanked by tall, slender minarets. The Persian-influenced arches, finely detailed chajja (overhanging eave), and trefoil wall cresting, all contribute to its rich and intricate design and ornamentation.

Fig 85: Bilal mosque, Bijapur

Bilal Mosque follows a rectangular plan and features a triple-arched façade, flanked by tall minarets, with a decorative chajja and arch-head cresting, a quintessential example of a typical Adil Shahi mosque.

Mosque Architecture in Bijapur

Most mosques during the Adil Shahi period in Bijapur were generally small, rectangular structures built using locally available basalt stone. These mosques reflect a fusion of Persian and Deccan styles, with distinct decorative elements introduced during the period.

1) **Triple-Arched Façade**: It is a defining feature in many Adil Shahi mosques, where the entrance is composed of three adjacent arches.

2) **Chajjas & Wall Cresting**: It is prominent from the beginning of the Adil Shahi rule. Chajjas (projected eave) vary in design, while wall cresting (decorative pattern along the top of a wall or arch) includes arch-head and trefoil patterns.

3) **Arches**: Characterized by strong Persian influence, these include both pointed and ogee arches. An ogee arch is formed by two opposing S-shaped curves that create a graceful, flowing outline. The Adil Shahi arches are often enhanced by a decorative floral motif at its crown.

Fig 86:Pointed Arch (the large main arch framing the central niche) and Ogee arch (the smaller decorative arch within the niche) at Jami Masjid, Bijapur, with a decorative floral motif at its crown.

Fig 87: Makka Masjid, Bijapur
The Mosque was used by the royal ladies during the Adil shah reign.

4) **Minarets**: Most mosques feature tall, decorative minarets flanking the façade, though in some cases they appear as smaller, bulbous cupolas on all four corners. (example: Makka masjid) Much like those in Safavid architecture, these minarets served an aesthetic purpose rather than a functional one.

5) **Domes**: Most mosques feature bulbous or onion-shaped domes, with foliation at the base that creates the impression of a bud encircled by petals.

6) **Ablution Tanks**: Typically located in front of the mosque and is used for ritual purification.

Fig 88: Mosque in Bijapur
It features the onion shaped dome with foliation at the base that creates the impression of a bud encircled by petals.

Fig 89: Malik Jahaan Begam Mosque, Bijapur

Fig 90: Safa Masjid, 2009

Chapter 6

Mosques in Goa: Safa Masjid—History, Features, Drawings

Having explored the rich history of the Adil Shahi dynasty and the ideas that shaped their architecture, we now turn our attention to the mosques they built in Goa, particularly Safa Masjid. The following chapters explores how these mosques adapted to the local landscape and climate, the influences they drew upon in their architecture and how these choices resonate with the way they ruled their kingdom.

Historical accounts suggest that over 27 mosques once stood in Ponda during the Adil Shah reign, but it is believed only Safa Masjid has survived. Its highly decorative stone plinth, elegant arches and large water tank indicate that it was a prominent mosque. The presence of a minbar (pulpit) typically signifies a Friday congregational mosque, though this is not always the case. The open grounds surrounding the mosque suggest that it may have also served as an Idgah. Illustrations from Lopes Mendes's book (1886) depict most of the mosques in Goa as modest structures, with no much detailing or elevated plinths. In contrast, Safa Masjid stands apart, its high plinth and architectural features, highlighting its significance. This might explain why it escaped destruction by the Portuguese and subsequent Hindu rulers, as it remained a cherished symbol of the Muslim community. Even today, Safa Masjid comes alive during festivals, gathering large crowds and celebrating its rich history.

Fig 91: Site Plan of Safa Masjid

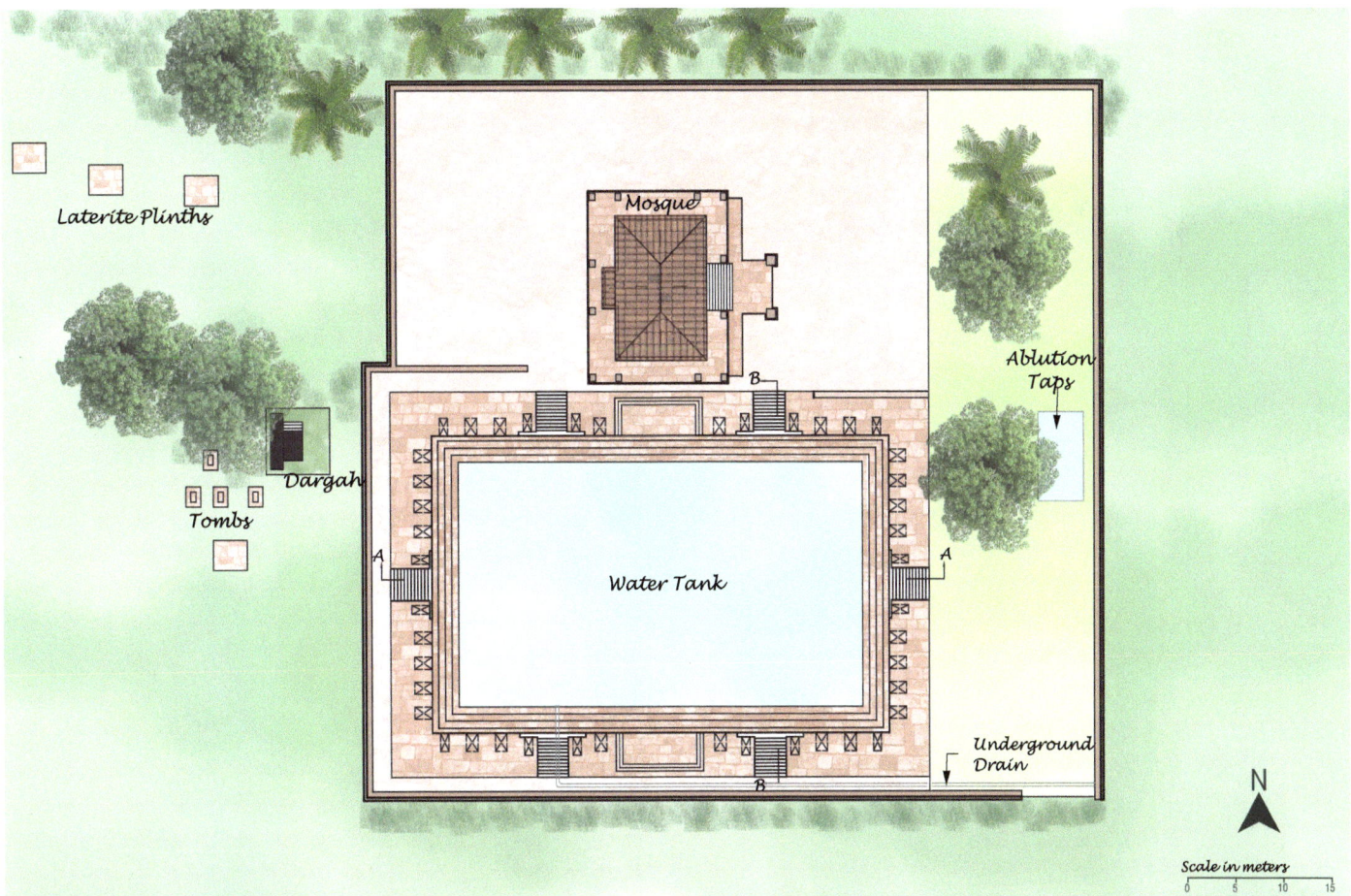

Fig 92: Safa Masjid Site Overview, 2009

Safa Masjid

Safa Masjid could be a scene from a postcard, it stands silently on a laterite plinth, the sloping roof sheltering the mosque on all four sides, while the vast blue sky drapes over it, enveloping the entire scene in its embrace.

The mosque is adorned with Persian influenced ogee arches on all sides, their curves like outstretched arms, reaching towards the sky in a silent prayer. The water tank seemed discreet from a distance, but at closer view, it reveals itself as an expansive lake. The tank is encircled by ogee arched niches, like a crown, broken by staircases along its peripheries.

The mosque stands modest, its single prayer hall spanning 13.8 by 8.8 meters. A flight of stairs ascends to a 2.4 meter high plinth, lifting the mosque gently above the earth. The walls, 60 centimeters thick, bear the weight of time.

I had first visited Safa Masjid in 2009, during my thesis project. Fifteen years later, in December 2024, I returned, and the mosque still had the same mesmerizing effect on me.

Although women are not allowed inside the mosque, I stood outside, peering through the entrance and felt a sense of tranquillity. The interior design echoes its exterior, with triple-arched façades mirrored on all four sides. The mihrab is crowned by arch head cresting and framed by two graceful pilasters.

The Imam, back in 2009, recalled a time when the mosque floor was paved with laterite stone, a trace to the Adil Shahi era. Today it has been replaced with vitrified tiles, a change brought about by the Archaeological Survey of India, Goa circle. The roof is covered with tiles, supported by a wooden framework.

The mosque has witnessed generations pass through its doors, listening in silence to countless heartfelt prayers whispered within its walls.

Fig 93: Safa masjid Frontal View, 2024

The entire mosque, along with its decorative laterite plinth, rests on a 40-centimeter-high platform, encircled by 14 octagonal laterite pillars. These pillars are set on sturdy square stone platforms measuring 80 x 80 cm. It is likely that a sheltered colonnade once ran around the mosque, offering protection from the intense summer heat and heavy monsoon rains.

The sloping roof, reminiscent of vernacular Goan architecture, suggests an adaptation to the local environment. The craftsmanship reflects the skill of local artisans who employed traditional construction methods suited to the region's climate and materials.

However, there are no historical records confirming whether this was the mosque's original roof or a later addition during the Adil Shah period. The earliest known illustration, dating to the late 19th century, almost 200 years after Adil Shah's rule in Goa, depicts Safa Masjid in a partially ruined state. (see Fig. 141, pg 94).

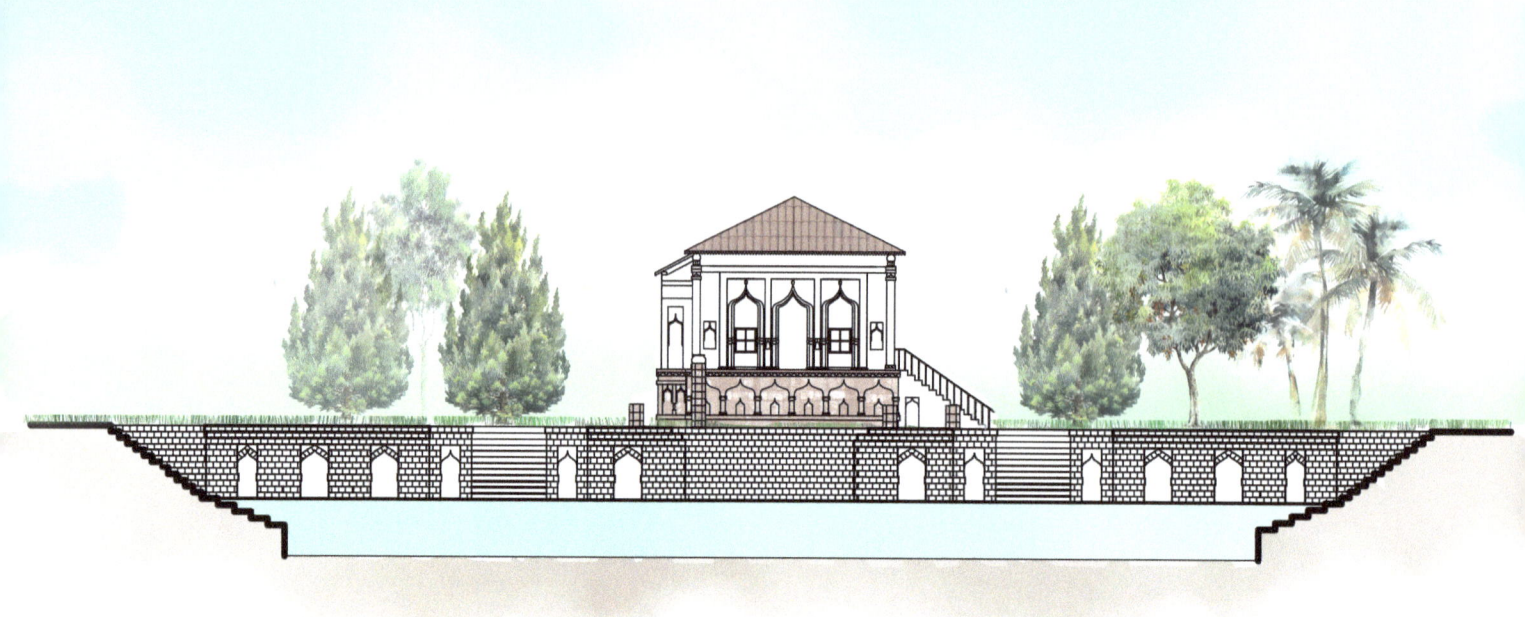

Section AA

Fig 94: Longitudinal Site Section of Safa Masjid

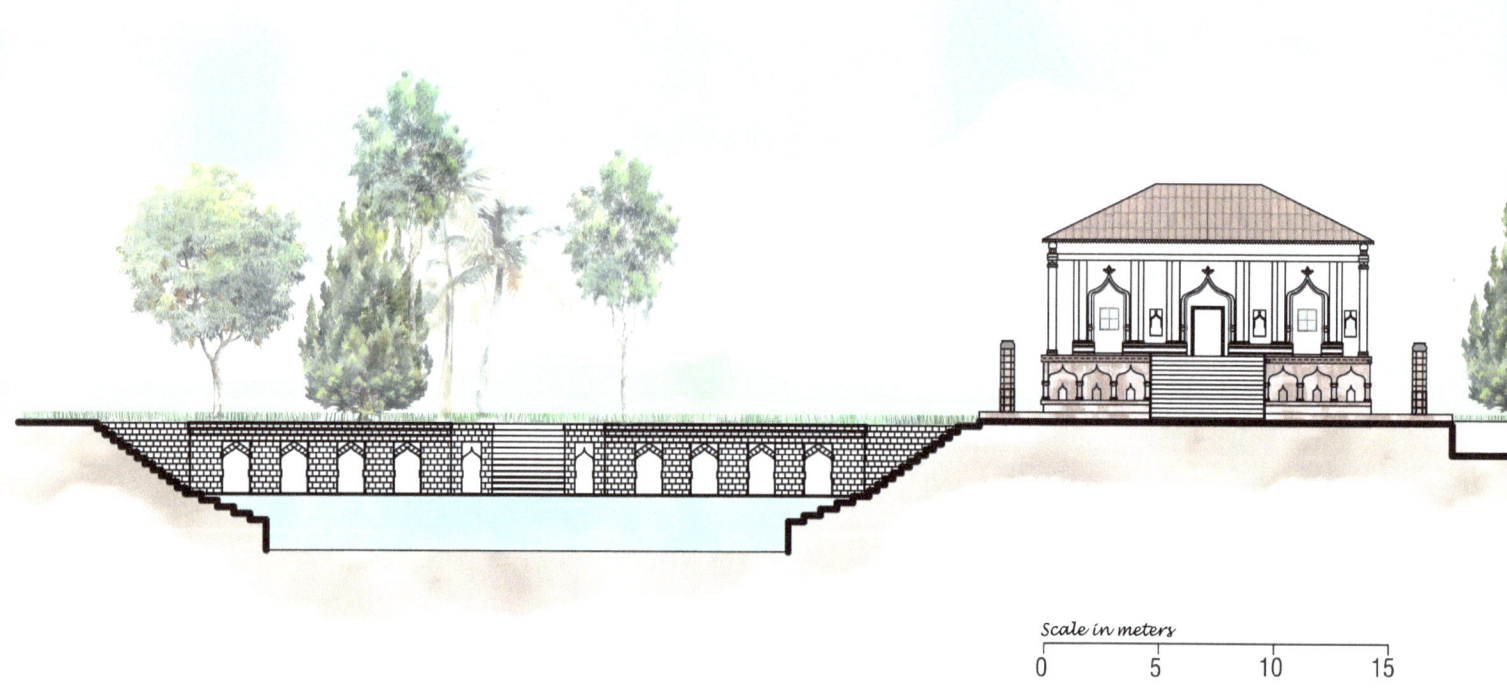

Section BB

Fig 95: Transverse Site Section of Safa Masjid

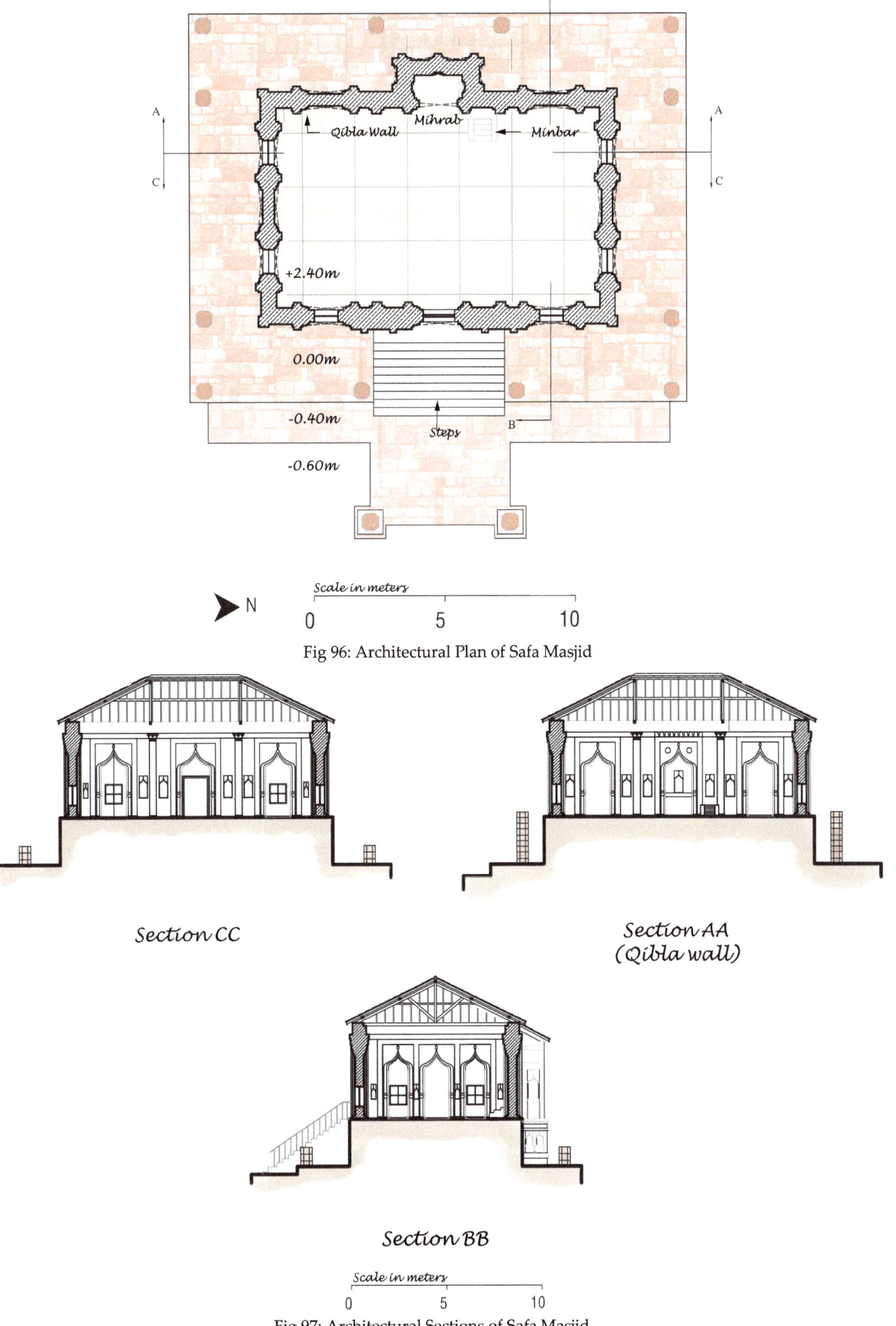

Fig 96: Architectural Plan of Safa Masjid

Section CC

Section AA (Qibla wall)

Section BB

Fig 97: Architectural Sections of Safa Masjid

Fig 98: Dargah at Safa Masjid

Dargahs

Dargahs are prevalent in Bijapur and are also found in Goa. For example, the dargah of Ghazi Abdullah Khan Shahid in Ponda, Khwaja Ismail Chishti (Konadi Dargah) in Pernem and Hazrat Mohammad Hamza Shah Dargah in Bardez.

Safa Masjid is also associated with a Dargah. To the west of the water tank lies the Dargah of Hazrat Abdul Rehman Qureshi, along with smaller tombs.

Fig 99: Dargah of Hazrat Abdul Rehman Qureshi, Safa Masjid

Fig 100: Family Tomb at Safa Masjid

Fig 101: Tomb near Dargah, Safa Masjid

Fig 102: Tombs at Safa Masjid

Fig 103: One of the Laterite Plinths at Safa Masjid

Tombs In The Vicinity

Next to the Dargah within the Safa Masjid complex, several tombs made of laterite stone are seen. While there are no historical records confirming their origins, the tombs feature the similar Persian-style ogee arch in the center carved into the tomb stone. Historical references, such as Lopes Mendes's illustration of a mosque in Sanquelim, (see fig 139, pg 92) also show tombs located near the mosque, supporting the tradition of burials near places of worship.

It is possible that these tombs belonged to the disciples of a Sufi saint, following the common practice of burying followers near their spiritual guide. They could also be the tombs of governors or other important figures from the region. In many cases, tombs built on a shared plinth indicate a family burial site, a practice seen in royal mausoleums like Ibrahim Rauza and Gol Gumbaz, where rulers were laid to rest alongside their families.

To the west of the masjid, near the tombs there are small decorative laterite plinths, similar in design to Safa Masjid. These plinths are noticeably smaller and lower in height. The structures that once rose above them have not withstood the test of time. They may once have served as retreats for Sufi mystics, offering a peaceful space for meditation and prayer, yet today only the mysterious, age-old plinths remain.

The Enigma of Safa Masjid's Origins

The origins of Safa Masjid remain veiled in mystery, its history entangled in a web of dates and rulers. It is commonly believed that the mosque was commissioned in 1560 by Ibrahim Adil Shah I, acting through his trusted governor Asad Khan. However, this timeline raises intriguing questions.

Ibrahim Adil Shah I ruled from 1534 to 1557, and Asad Khan is believed to have died around 1549,[67] making it unlikely that either could have overseen a mosque built in 1560. If their involvement is to be accepted, then the mosque must have been constructed earlier, possibly between 1530s to 1540s.

In an alternate theory, Dr. M. A. Nayeem, in his book Heritage of the Adil Shahis of Bijapur, attributes the construction of the Safa Masjid to Ismail Adil Shah in 1518, suggesting it was built earlier by the predecessor of Ibrahim Adil Shah I.[68]

There is inscriptional evidence from a similarly named Masjid-i-Safa in Belgaum. Records state that Asad Khan, then governor of Belgaum, laid the foundation of that mosque in 1518 and donated land to it in 1519. The interior of the mosque is notable for its use of rows of reused temple columns, reflecting the adaptive architectural practices of the time. While this is a different structure from the Safa Masjid in Ponda, certain features, such as the absence of a dome, its white colour, the similarity in name, bear a striking resemblance.

However, the most persuasive attribution lies with Ali Adil Shah I. George Michell and Mark Zebrowski, in Architecture and Art of the Deccan Sultanates refer to a "Safa Shahuri mosque" built in 1560 at Ponda, attributing it to the reign of Ali Adil Shah I (1558–1580),[69] a ruler noted for his ambitious building campaigns. His reign was marked by an ambitious wave of architectural activity, alongside substantial advancements in the water system. He commissioned several significant structures and palaces in Bijapur, like the Anand and Gagan Mahal, the impressive Jami Masjid which was the principal mosque of the city in Bijapur, and Chand Bawadi, a grand community water tank built in memory of his beloved wife. Given his enthusiasm for construction and water system, it is entirely possible that Safa Masjid was one of his contributions.

Dating the Safa Masjid to the reign of Ali Adil Shah's successor, Ibrahim Adil Shah II, is unlikely. His architectural style is marked by elaborate calligraphic inscriptions and intricate ornamentation, features that are absent from the Safa Masjid.

Large, engineered water tanks were not commonly constructed during the reign of Ismail Adil Shah, as the development of bawadis gained momentum during the reign of Ibrahim Adil Shah I.

But the most extensive phase of infrastructural and architectural activity, particularly the advancement in waterworks occurred under Ali Adil Shah I, especially following the Battle of Talikota in 1565, where the victory brought wealth and resources to Bijapur.

The construction of such an expansive tank at Safa Masjid, despite Goa not being the Adil Shahs' capital, reflects the prosperity of Bijapur at the time and the dynasty's ability to fund major developments in Goa.

Fig 104: Safa Masjid, Belagavi (Belgaum)
Photo from Wikimedia Cmmons, Public Domain

Front Elevation

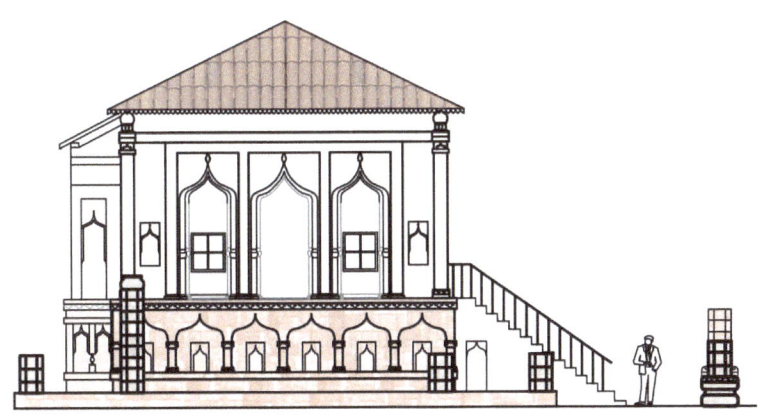

North Side Elevation

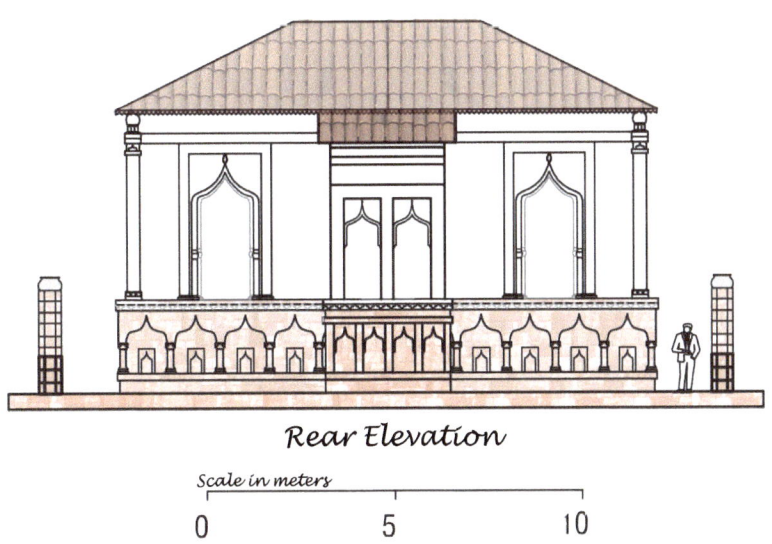

Rear Elevation

Fig 105: Elevation Drawings of Safa Masjid

Fig 106: Safa masjid Frontal View, 2009

Bijapur Architectural Influence on Safa Masjid

Several architectural features of Safa Masjid share similarities with mosques in Bijapur. Below are some of the most notable and distinct elements that reflect this connection.

Triple arched façade

The triple arched façade is a characteristic feature of many mosques in Bijapur. Most of these mosques are small and rectangular, often featuring pointed ogee arches similar to those of Safa Masjid.

Minarets

Upon closer inspection of Safa Masjid, small, bulbous-like projections can be seen at each of the four corners. These are minarets, a distinctive feature of Adil Shahi architecture. The Adil Shahis often attached minarets to mosque walls, varying in form from tall and slender to shorter, bulbous shapes, as seen at Safa Masjid.

Raised Plinth

Many prominent mosques in Bijapur are built on elevated plinths, emphasizing their significance and architectural grandeur. Similarly, Safa Masjid stands on a raised plinth, featuring beautifully carved laterite ogee arches highlighting its importance and beauty.

Pilasters

Inside Safa Masjid, pilasters stand between arches. In Bijapur, I have rarely come across pilasters in mosques or mausoleums. The only exception being Ibrahim Rauza, the mausoleum of Ibrahim Adil Shah II, where pilasters topped with corbels stand between arches adorned with intricate calligraphy. His tomb's façade includes pilasters, (see fig.107)

Fig 107: Calligraphy and Pilasters at Ibrahim Rauza
Photo by Ashwin Kumar Flickr (CC BY-SA 2.0)

a design element more commonly seen on church facades, temples and heritage structures in Goa during the Portuguese reign. Notably, the design on the capital of the pilaster at Ibrahim Rauza closely resembles that of Safa Masjid.

Fig 108: Pilasters on the Mihrab Wall, Safa Masjid

Fig 109: Qibla Wall, Safa Masjid

Fig 110: Safa Masjid in a yellow hue, 2024

Safa Masjid-The Name

The name Safa Masjid also known as Shahouri Masjid may have historical and linguistic roots, possibly reflecting cultural and royal influences. The term Shahouri is not widely documented, but it could be linked to the Persian word Shahr (meaning "city") or Shah (meaning "king"). If Shahouri is derived from Shahr, it might indicate that the mosque was considered a significant city mosque or one associated with royal patronage.

The word Safa means "pure" in Arabic, reflecting the spiritual essence of the mosque. It is tempting to speculate that the name Safa Masjid may also have been influenced by the Safavid dynasty. While there is no definitive evidence in the name, the Adil Shah rulers maintained strong ties with Persia, and Persian architectural and cultural influences were prominent in Bijapur. Whether the word Safa was inspired by the Safavid legacy or not, the possibility remains intriguing.

Safa Masjid was maintained and preserved by the local community until 1968. In that year, it was declared a national monument and entrusted under the care of the Archaeological Survey of India (ASI).[70] While no historical records confirm its original colour, Safa Masjid had traditionally been white. However, during a recent visit in 2024, I observed that it had been repainted in a creamish-yellow hue. When questioned, ASI officials provided no definitive explanation for the change. This alteration raises concerns about the need for greater transparency in conservation efforts.

Fig 111: Approach to Safa Masjid from the Road, 2024

The National Highway's Impact

The construction of a national highway bypass in close proximity to Safa Masjid has had a direct and troubling impact on this important heritage site. Built without adequate consideration for the mosque's historical and cultural significance, the new road has not only reduced the mosque's visibility and accessibility but also contributed to physical damage.

Vibrations from the constant movement of heavy vehicles along the bypass have reportedly weakened the walls of the mosque's water tank. According to reports in The Times of India (July 2021) and O Heraldo (Feburary 2024), Murtuza Mulla, president of the Safa Masjid committee, stated that these vibrations have caused visible cracks and structural damage to the tank. The Archaeological Survey of India (ASI) has since undertaken repair work to address cracks and structural damage to the Safa Masjid water tank.[71]

When I visited Safa Masjid in December 2024, the impact was immediately evident. I had to stop and ask for directions to find the mosque. A place once central and prominent, now quite literally bypassed.

During the monsoon season this year (2025), Safa Masjid's lawns and tank were flooded by water gushing directly from the road into the mosque's premises.[71a]

This experience reflects a broader concern, the increasing threat that modern infrastructure poses to our cultural heritage when development is prioritised without proper planning or preservation in mind.

Chapter 7

Mosques in Goa: Surla Masjid—History, Features, Drawings

While researching Safa Masjid, I came across another mosque from the Adil Shah period—Surla Masjid, located in the village of Tar Surla in Bicholim Taluka. It is set at the foothills and lies along the banks of a tributary of the River Mandovi. It is now maintained by the Directorate of Archives and Archaeology, Goa.

The exact date of Surla Masjid's construction remains unknown, though it is believed to have been built in the early to mid-16th century, possibly around the same time or even before the Safa Masjid. The mosque is relatively modest in size, measuring 12.4 meters by 10.2 meters, and constructed from 60 cm thick laterite stone.

Fig 112: View of Surla Masjid, 2024

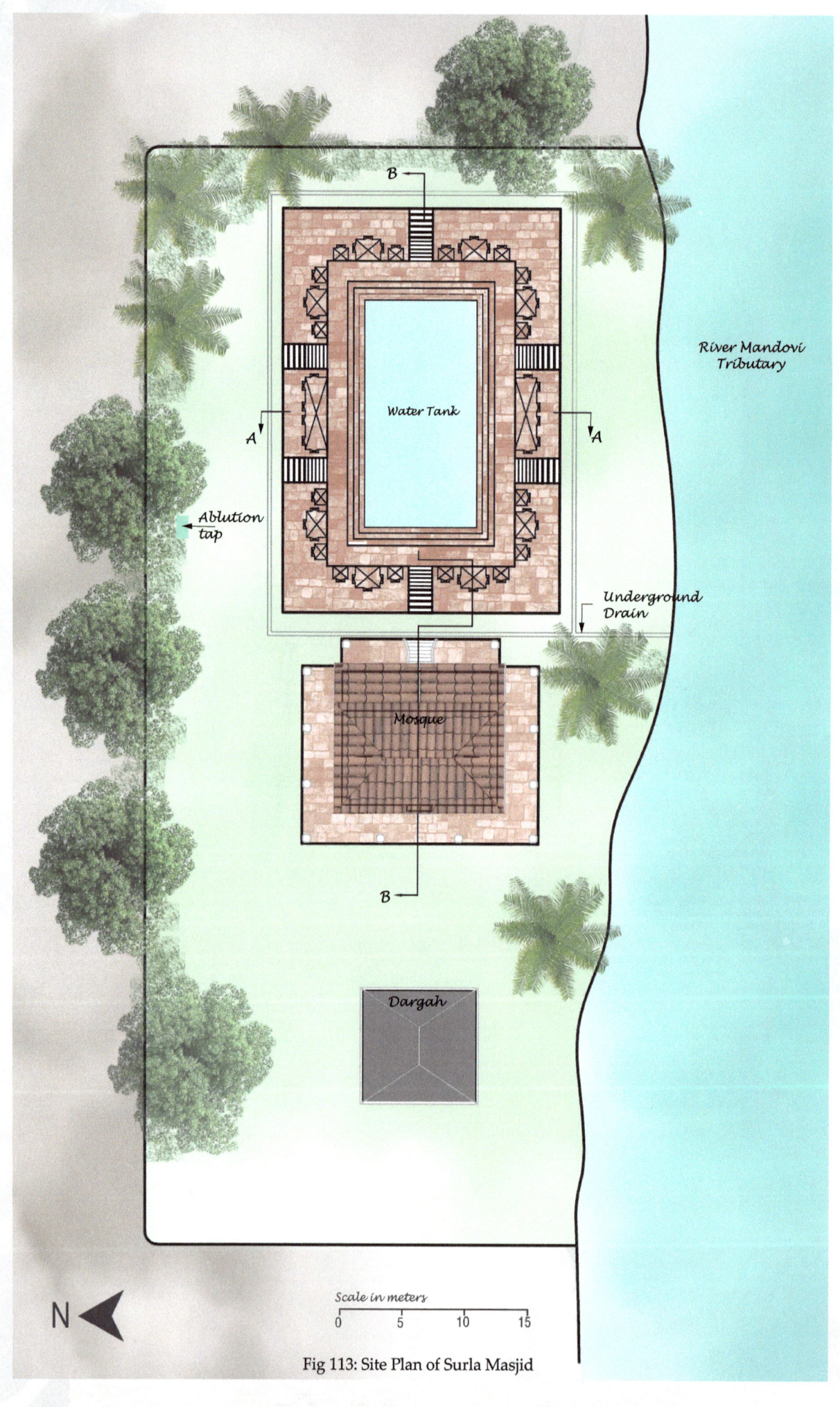

Fig 113: Site Plan of Surla Masjid

Section BB

Fig 114: Longitudinal Site Section of Surla Masjid

Section AA

Fig 115: Transverse Site Section of Surla Masjid

Fig 116: View of Surla Masjid, 2024

Fig 117: Surla Masjid Prayer Hall, 2024

Before entering the prayer hall, one ascends a flight of stairs, encountering a transition space approximately 2.4 meters wide. While the exact purpose of this space remains unclear, the steps leading from the transition space to the prayer hall bears resemblance to the steps found in traditional Goan homes.

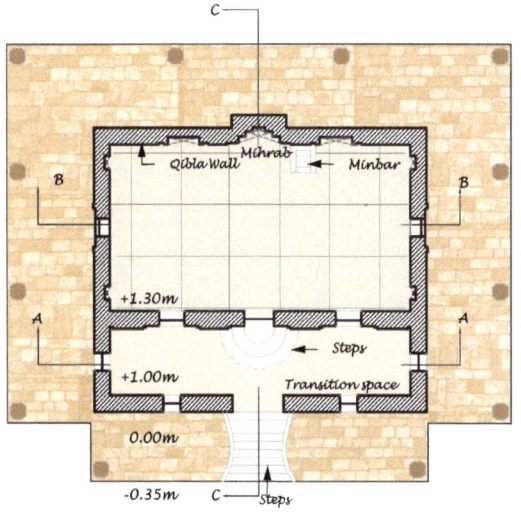

Fig 118: Transition Space Before Prayer Hall, Surla Masjid, 2024

Fig 119: Architectural Plan of Surla Masjid

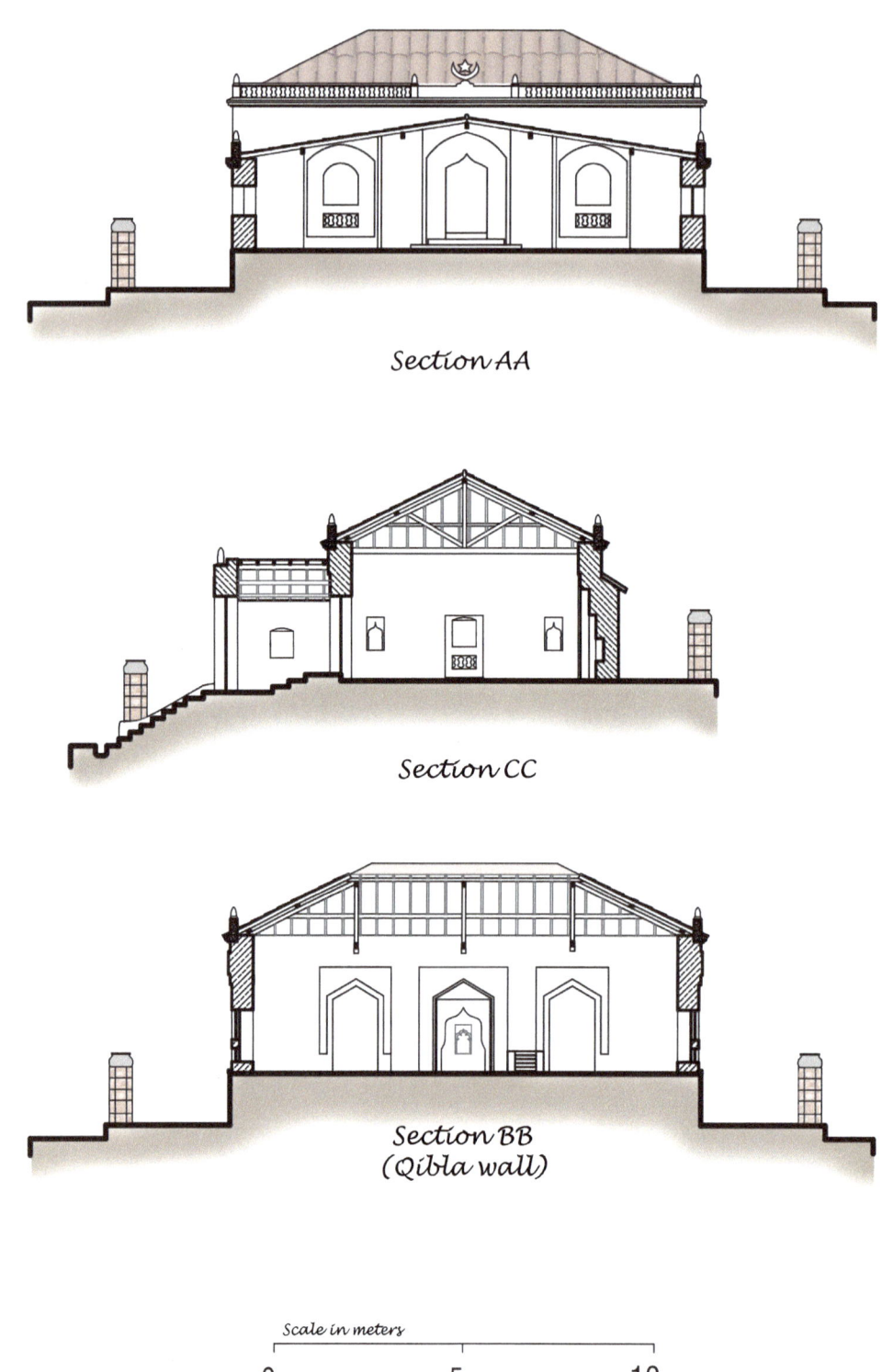

Fig 120: Architectural Sections of Surla Masjid

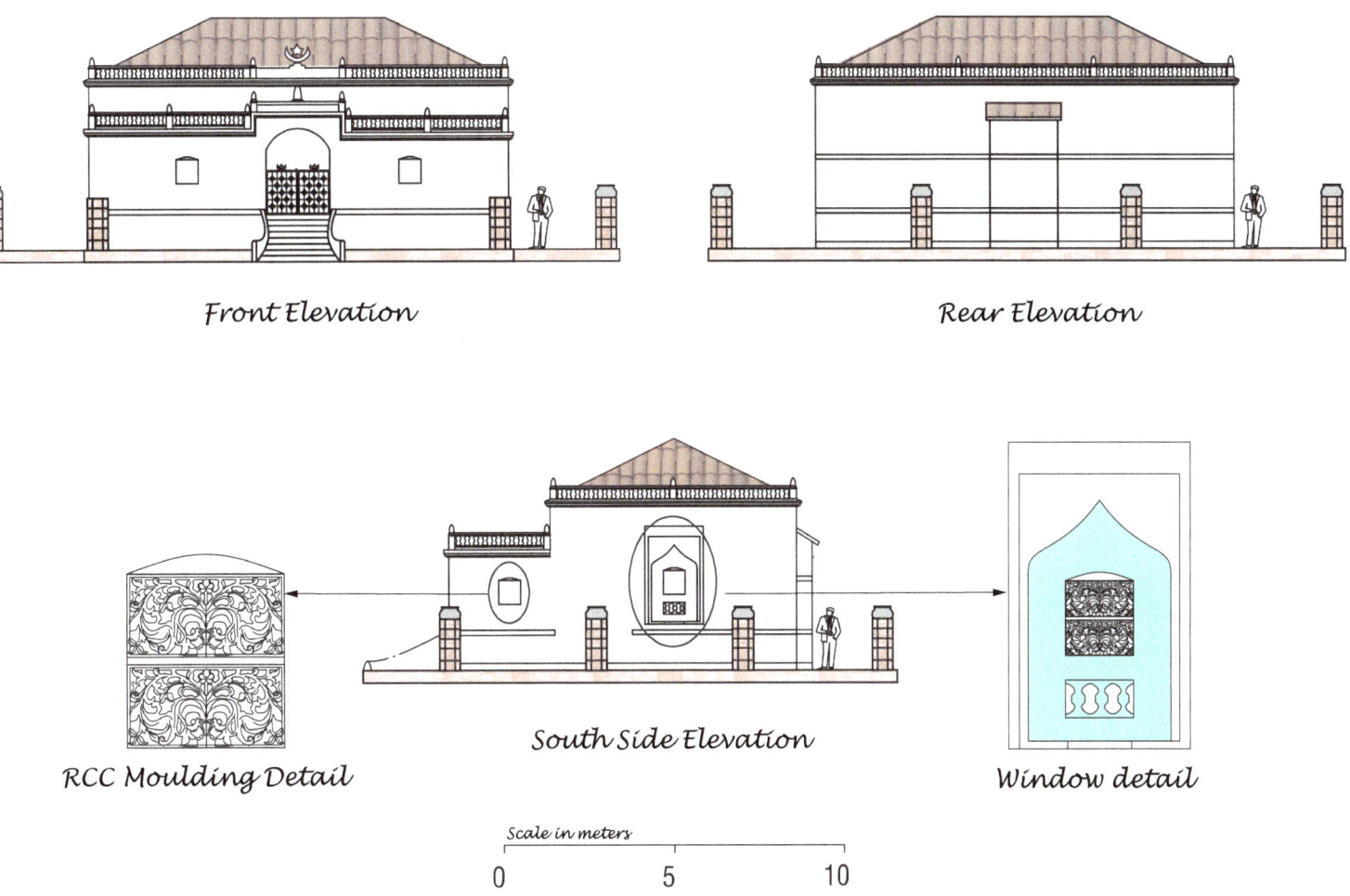

Fig 121: Elevation Drawings of Surla Masjid

Surla Masjid is elevated on a 35 cm high platform and encircled by twelve octagonal laterite pillars, each capped with a round black metal (iron) top. Similar pillars can be seen around Safa Masjid. While their exact purpose remains uncertain, it is unlikely that they served merely as aesthetic features or symbolic minarets, as such elements were not common in Deccan mosque architecture. Instead, their placement suggests that they were once part of a colonnade supporting a roofed structure. Over time, the roof may have deteriorated, leaving only these structural traces standing.

The mosque's side elevations features arched openings adorned with decorative *jali* (screen), made of RCC (reinforced cement concrete) mouldings and balusters, which appears to be a later modification. The front façade of Surla Masjid is comparatively simple, lacking the triple-arched design of Safa Masjid. Instead, it presents a semi-circular arched entrance flanked by two small openings. The mosque is crowned with a four-way sloping roof, covered in tiles and supported by a wooden framework.

Fig 122: Mihrab of Surla Masjid

Fig 124: Mihrab of Safa Masjid

The mihrab projection of the Surla Masjid is covered by a single way sloping roof, similar to that of the Safa Masjid. However, this single-sloped roof appears to be a later addition. In Adil Shahi mosques, the mihrab which is the most sacred element of a mosque, was always given prominence, often marked by an ornate dome or intricate detailing. In Bijapur, Adil Shahi mosques consistently emphasized this space, highlighting its religious and architectural importance. The simple, single-sloped roof over the mihrab at Surla and Safa Masjid deviates from this tradition, suggesting it may have been a later modification rather than part of the mosque's original design.

Fig 123: Exterior Mihrab projection, Surla Masjid

Fig 125: Exterior Mihrab projection, Safa Masjid

Fig 126: Frontal View of Surla Masjid, 2024

Aligned with the mosque of Surla Masjid is the dargah of Hazrat Pir Saheb, which forms part of the larger religious complex. The Dargah is venerated by both muslims and Hindus.

Surla Masjid shares a few similarities with Safa Masjid and mosques in Bijapur. All these structures are small and rectangular in plan and feature a water tank and dargah in the vicinity. However, despite these common elements, Surla Masjid remains more modest compared to Safa Masjid and the grander mosques of Bijapur.

Fig 127: Dargah of Hazrat Pir Saheb, Surla Masjid

Climate and Materials

Bijapur experiences relatively low rainfall, while Goa faces heavy monsoon rains, which must have made it challenging to construct and maintain domes during the Adil shahi period, leading to the adoption of sloping roofs in both Safa and Surla Masjid.

Mosques in Bijapur were constructed from sturdy basalt stone, while Safa and Surla Masjid in Goa were built using easily carvable laterite stone. This softer material not only suited the local climate but also allowed for decorative elements, such as the detailed plinth of Safa Masjid and the arches in both water tanks.

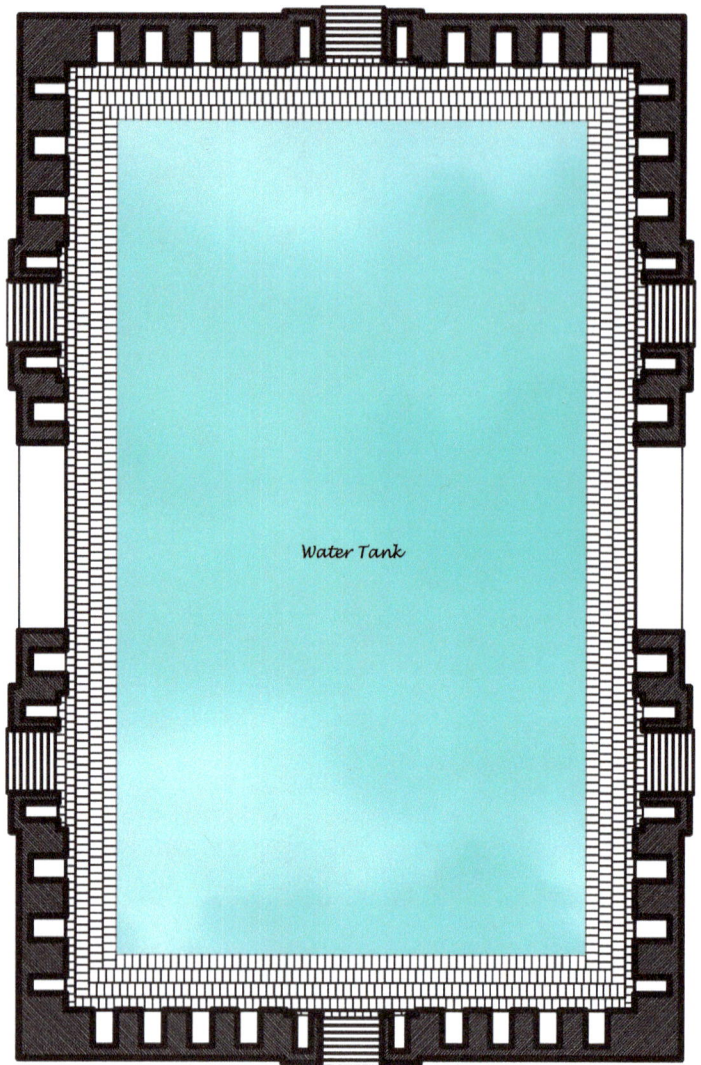

Fig 128: Architectural Plan of Safa and Surla Water Tanks

The Water Tanks In Goa

Safa Masjid Water Tank

The water tank is situated to the south of the mosque and spans an impressive 1,410 square meters, nearly 12 times the area of the mosque itself. The tank has natural springs, ensuring it remains filled throughout the year.

The water tank at Safa Masjid measures approximately, 55 meters in length and 38 meters in breadth, with six flights of steps, 3 meters wide, leading down to the water level. The tank has a depth of approximately 5 meters.

The water tank features ogee pointed arches measuring 2.2 meters by 1.2 meters, which are reminiscent of Persian architectural styles. These arches are recessed into the wall, forming niches with a depth of 1.8 meters.

Goa served as a pleasure retreat for the Adil Shah rulers, who had a deep appreciation for gardens and parks. It is likely that the tank was used in maintaining these green spaces. The presence of deep niches within the tank suggests that it may have also functioned as a place for socializing and relaxation, contributing to the leisurely atmosphere of the time. Being associated with a mosque, the tank also held religious significance, providing water for ablution (ritual purification), a practice that continues to this day.

Fig 129: Safa Masjid Water tank, 2009

The water tank remains calm and still, only ruffles when people use its pristine water to cleanse themselves before entering the mosque. The mosque is surrounded by manicured gardens.

Left: Fig 130: Although ablution taps were provided, men are seen performing ablution using the traditional water source, 2009.

Below: Fig 131: Women are seen collecting water for household use, 2009

Fig 132: Surla Masjid Water Tank, 2024

Surla Masjid Water Tank

In contrast to the water tank at Safa Masjid, the Surla Masjid's tank is situated in front of the mosque. Its size is less than one-quarter that of the Safa Masjid tank, and is adorned with recessed arched niches around its perimeter. The tank measures 23 meters in length and 15 meters in width, with six flights of steps, each 1.9 meters wide, leading to the water level. The depth of the tank is approximately 1 meter. The water in the tank is collected from the surrounding hills through natural gravity.

The arches surrounding the tank at Surla Masjid are ogee pointed arches, similar in style to those found at the Safa Masjid tank. However, the arches at Surla are significantly larger and more deeply set. These are not just shallow niches but function more like enclosed rooms. Some of the smaller spaces measure around 1.5 square meters, while the larger ones extend up to 40 square meters in area.

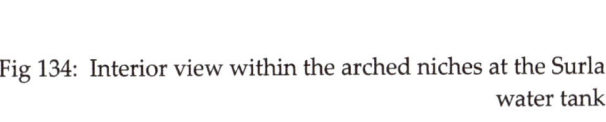

Fig 133: Surla Masjid Water Tank from Arches, 2024

During the Adil Shah period, this site likely served as a resting place for traders travelling to the port at Panjim. The arch-shaped niches surrounding the water tank may have served as resting spots for travelling merchants, offering them a designated pause along their route to the main port. (Imam of Surla Masjid, personal communication, 2009)

The water tanks at Surla Masjid and Safa Masjid share a similar concept with the tanks of Bijapur with its large niches designed as resting and community spaces, reflecting the architectural influence of Bijapur's bawadis.

Fig 134: Interior view within the arched niches at the Surla water tank

Chapter 8

The Forgotten Inheritance: The Adil Shahs and Us

The possibility of a dome at Safa Masjid

Did the Safa Masjid always have a sloping roof? This question has lingered in my mind for some time. While there's no definitive historical record to confirm its original form, several architectural clues suggest that a dome may once have crowned the mosque, now lost to time due to climate or conflict.

The Adil Shahs, who built the mosque in the 16th century, were renowned patrons of art and architecture. Their buildings in Bijapur, such as the grand Gol Gumbaz, are celebrated for their scale and elegance, especially their domes. It is hard to imagine that a dynasty known for such monumental domed structures would have built a mosque as modest as Safa Masjid appears today.

Goa's heavy monsoon climate may have necessitated the addition of a sloping roof at some point in the mosque's life. While practical, the current roof feels like a later intervention rather than an original design.

- The plain frieze, for example, contrasts sharply with the ornate friezes with cresting and chajjas, typical of Adil Shahi mosques. This visual inconsistency suggests that

Fig 135: Interpreted Illustration of Safa Masjid with a Dome

the upper portion of the mosque may have been rebuilt or altered, perhaps after the original dome was damaged.
- In typical Adil Shahi architecture, the mihrab (Prayer niche) is often emphasized with a dome or decorative niche to mark its sacred significance. At Safa Masjid, however, the area above the mihrab is covered by a single, sloping roof that feels abrupt and architecturally disconnected.
- The decorative laterite plinth of Safa Masjid resembles the architectural detailing found on the masjid water tank, suggesting that both were likely constructed during the same timeline. However, the mosque that now stands above it, with its simple sloping roof and open interior layout bears little architectural continuity with the richly worked base. This kind of stylistic disconnect between plinth and superstructure is highly unusual in Adil Shahi architecture, where design elements typically flow in a cohesive manner from the foundation to the roofline.

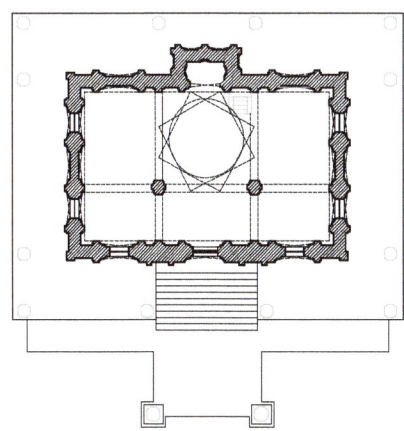

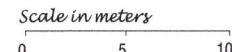

Fig 136: Hypothetical Plan of Safa Masjid with a Central Dome

Fig 137: Hypothetical reconstruction of Safa Masjid featuring a central dome and encircling sloped portico

- Adding to this mystery is the absence of inscriptions, a striking detail, considering that dedicatory or commemorative texts were common in major Islamic structures of that time. The lack of any dates or inscriptions may indicate that the original mosque was destroyed, possibly during the Maratha invasions or Portuguese expansion, and later rebuilt by the local Muslim community.
- The absence of a dome, ornamental friezes, points to a significant break from established Adil Shahi architectural conventions. The original structure may have included interior columns supporting a central dome, which would align more closely with typical Adil Shahi mosque architecture. Fully open-plan mosques, like the current layout at Safa are extremely rare in Bijapur-era construction, where domes, arches and internal supports were key spatial elements.
- Another possibility is that Safa Masjid originally had a flat roof. Although rare, a few flat-roofed mosques were built during the Adil Shahi period, one example being the Ibrahim's old Jami Masjid, attributed to Ibrahim Adil Shah I. However, this raises an important question: if the intention was to use a simple roof form, why opt for a flat roof, especially in Goa's heavy monsoon climate, where a pitched or sloped roof would have been far more practical. If the flat roof was part of the original design, it doesn't quite fit with the local climate or the practical approach usually seen in Adil Shahi architecture.

The Adil Shahs, who ruled much of the Deccan, were skilled builders known for their advanced architectural achievements. They constructed Gol Gumbaz, one of the largest domes in the world, and engineered the floating ceiling at Ibrahim Rauza. Many of their structures feature domes and they employed architects and craftsmen from Persia and beyond who brought with them rich traditions in Islamic architecture.

Taken together, these clues build a strong case that Safa Masjid may have originally had a dome. The features we see today could be the result of later changes, repairs or adaptations made over time. The mosque's architecture still hints at a richer, more layered past. While nothing is certain, and no definitive evidence has yet confirmed it. The question remains open, an unresolved piece of history that invites further exploration.

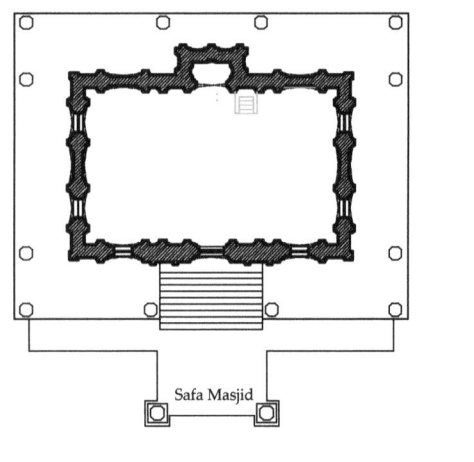

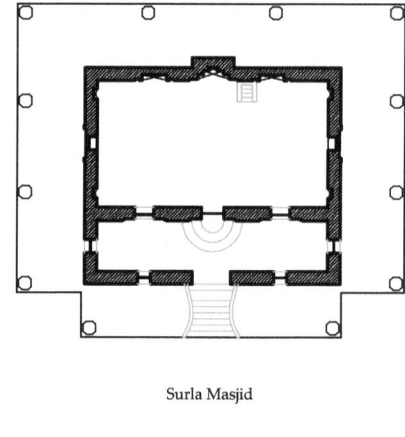

Fig 138: Comparative Plans of Safa Masjid (*left*), Surla Masjid (*right*), and a Typical Bijapur Mosque (*middle*)

When comparing the plans of Safa Masjid, Surla Masjid and a typical Adil Shahi mosque in Bijapur, certain patterns begin to emerge. All three mosques share a comparable scale and rectangular layout, suggesting a common architectural design within the Adil Shahi period. However, important distinctions raise questions about the original form and evolution of Safa Masjid. Mosques designed with a fully open interior layout, like the current form of Safa, are highly uncommon in constructions from the Bijapur period, which was generally characterised by the use of domes, arches, as main architectural components.

In contrast, Surla Masjid features a transition space, resembling the entrance layout of traditional Goan homes. The presence of laterite pillars surrounding both Goan mosques is a distinctive feature not commonly found in Bijapur mosques. This architectural adaptation may reflect a response to Goa's torrential monsoon climate. The use of locally available laterite stone also highlights regional building practices.

Fig 139: Illustration of mosque in Sanquelim
By António Lopes Mendes, India Portuguesa, 1886

Mosque of the Moors in Sanquelim

In his accounts of colonised Goa, Lopes Mendes refers to a mosque in Sanquelim, which he describes as having insignificant architecture. He notes its presence after the Portuguese expansion of the New Conquests, mentioning it in the context of a festival celebrated by the Moors (Muslims). His observations suggest that the mosque was likely constructed by the local Muslim community, using vernacular architectural styles rather than royal patronage or monumental design.

Historically, Sanquelim remained under Adil Shah control until the mid-17th century, when it was seized by the Marathas and later taken over by the Bhosale dynasty of Sawantwadi.

The simplicity of the mosque's architecture, as described by Mendes, may reflect this late period built by locals during a time of shifting political rule and declining royal influence.

Interpreting the Amalgamated Architecture of Safa Masjid

There are several possible explanations for the original form and later changes to Safa Masjid, based on architectural clues, regional context and historical events.

One compelling theory is that the mosque originally featured a central dome, a common element in Adil Shahi architecture, along with a wraparound sloping roof supported by laterite columns. This sloped roof would have served a practical purpose by protecting worshippers from Goa's intense heat and heavy monsoon rains. A similar architectural arrangement is seen in the mosque illustrated in Karwar, documented in Lopes Mendes' drawings, where a central domed mosque is sheltered by an outer portico.

Over time, Safa Masjid's original structure may have been damaged or destroyed during military attacks in Ponda, a region that changed hands multiple times during the late Adil Shahi period. It is likely that only the lower portion of the mosque survived, that is the decorative laterite plinth and portico columns. These elements are still visible today and are notably more refined in craftsmanship than the superstructure above.

Following the destruction, it is likely that the local community rebuilt the mosque on the surviving base. While they may not have been able to replicate the original design and craftsmanship of the original builders, they made efforts to preserve key architectural features, such as the triple-arched façade and Persian arches. Simpler construction methods and locally available materials were used in the reconstruction of the mosque that resulted in the current mosque design, with a pitched, tiled roof, reflecting more of a regional building style than an Adil Shahi monument.

When Ponda eventually fell to the Portuguese in the late 18th century, the mosque may have likely suffered again, either through deliberate destruction, fire, or neglect. Given that the roof was constructed from lighter, perishable materials like timber and tile, it would have been especially vulnerable. In contrast, the laterite base and walls managed to survive.

It wasn't until the 1960s, when Safa Masjid came under the protection of the Archaeological Survey of India (ASI), that the roof was reconstructed, most likely based on regional precedents rather than original records. The current pitched roof, while functional, may not reflect the mosque's original form, and instead represents a layer in its long and complex history.

The mosque at the Fortress of Piro, (present-day Karwar) for example, had a dome topped with a crescent moon, and featured a triple-arched façade, arch head cresting, and corner finials, elements commonly found in Adil Shahi mosques in Bijapur. It also had a tiled portico supported by pillars, offering shelter from the harsh coastal climate. The presence of laterite pillar ruins at both Safa and Surla Masjid hints at a once-continuous colonnade, forming part of a more elaborate structure now lost.

Fig 140: Mosque of the Fortress of Piro, Karwar, Karnataka
By António Lopes Mendes, India Portuguesa, 1886

Fig 141 Illustration of Safa Masjid, *By António Lopes Mendes, India Portuguesa, 1886.*

Fig 142: View of Safa Masjid, 2024

Fig 143: Chand Bawadi, Bijapur

Comparing Adil Shahi Bawadis from Bijapur to Goa

The Adil Shahis were influenced by multiple sources in developing an advanced water management system in their capital. Their water system was a blend of Persian and Deccan Sultanate influences, adapted to suit Bijapur's semi-arid climate.

Bijapur faced challenges with limited rainfall, making water conservation crucial, as they were essential to sustaining both the urban population and monumental architecture.

Among the most significant elements of this water infrastructure were the bawadis. They are large water tanks designed to collect and store rainwater. These tanks played a vital role in ensuring a year-round water supply. The bawadis also enhanced the significance of monuments and were often strategically located near mosques, tombs and public structures. Many were named after the wives of the kings who commissioned them.

The 'bawadis' or water tanks were not only functional, but also served as social hubs where people could meet, rest and even perform ablutions before prayers.

Several significant bawadis were constructed during the Adil Shahi reign. Listed below are four prominent examples, each built by a successive Adil Shah ruler. These examples help us better understand the possible date, design and scale of the tanks found at Safa Masjid and Surla Masjid in Goa.

Ibrahimpur Bawadi (1534–1557)

Built by Ibrahim Adil Shah I in Ibrahimpur, during his reign between 1534–1557, it is believed to be one of the earliest bawadis of the Adil Shahi period.[72] It's a small tank, about one-third the size of the Safa Masjid tank. It has a series of arches around its edges, very similar to those at the Safa Masjid and Surla Masjid water tanks. Though small, it shows the early stages of water tank construction in Bijapur.

Chand Bawadi (1579)

Water tank construction increased and waterworks improved during the reign of Ali Adil Shah I (1557–1580). Chand Bawadi was built by him in 1579 and named after his wife,

Fig 144: Taj Bawadi, Bijapur

Chand Bibi. This tank later served as the inspiration for the Taj Bawadi, although the latter is much grander in both scale and design. Both structures feature an arch that leads to steps descending into the water. Chand Bawadi has rooms located on its southern side. The tank is associated with both a mosque and a tomb site (maqbara), similar to what is seen at Safa Masjid and Surla Masjid. Chand Bawadi is slightly larger than the Safa Masjid tank, approximately one-tenth bigger in size.

Taj Bawadi (1620)
Built by Ibrahim Adil Shah II(1580–1626) in memory of his wife, Taj Sultana, this is the grandest bawadi of them all. It has a huge entrance with a 35-foot arch and two octagonal towers topped with domes. This tank is almost three times the size of the Safa Masjid tank, showing the scale and ambition of royal projects at the time.

Masa Bawadi (1626–1656)
Believed to be constructed during the reign of Mohammed Adil Shah (1626–1656), the tank is located to the rear of his mausoleum, the renowned Gol Gumbaz.[73] Although limited historical and architectural records exist about the structure, it represents one of the last examples of large-scale water tanks under the Adil Shahs. Mohammed Adil Shah was the last powerful ruler of the dynasty. After his reign, during the rule of Ali Adil Shah II, the kingdom entered a period of decline, and the construction of monumental bawadis seems to have diminished.

Fig 145: Octagonal tower at Taj Bawadi , Bijapur

When we compare these Bijapur bawadis with the tanks at Safa Masjid and Surla Masjid in Goa, some interesting patterns come to light.

The Safa Masjid tank, which measures around 1410 square metres, is three times the size of Ibrahimpur Bawadi, but smaller than Chand Bawadi. Its size and design are more in line with Chand Bawadi, which suggests it may have been built during Ali Adil Shah's I reign.

It's important to remember that the Adil Shah kings did not reside in Goa permanently. The land and its buildings were overseen by governors appointed by the Bijapur court. This suggests that the Safa Masjid tank was likely commissioned by local governors. Given this, it seems unlikely that they would have commissioned a tank more expansive than those constructed under royal patronage in the capital. This adds weight to the idea that the Safa Masjid tank was built around the reign of Ali Adil Shah I, a period marked by increased prosperity and the construction of larger-scale bawadis, rather than during Ibrahim Adil Shah's I reign where the bawadis were smaller in scale.

As for Surla Masjid, it may date to the same period as Safa Masjid, or perhaps even earlier. The water tank at Surla is approximately about half the size of Ibrahimpur Bawadi in Bijapur. Its modest scale and remote location, set near the banks of a river, suggest that it was not intended for regular use by a settled community. Instead, it was likely meant to serve travelling merchants and passerby, functioning more as a resting point or temporary water resource than a central communal tank like Safa Masjid.

Fig 146: Ibrahim Adil Shah II Copper Coins
By JesúsGustavo (CC BY-SA 4.0)

Note: The above image does not depict the exact coins found in Goa, but serves as a general reference for coins issued during the reign of Ibrahim Adil Shah II.

A coin of Ibrahim II (1580-1626)and some coins of the Adil Shahi dynasty of later periods are seen in the Pilar Seminary Museum in Goa. These coins were collected from the Sanguem area which continued under the Adil shah dynasty till the 17th century.[74]

Ibrahim Adil Shah II, in particular, tried to promote cultural harmony through music, bridging divides between Shias and Sunnis, as well as Hindus and Muslims.

This emphasis on unity was complemented by their strategic foreign relations, which helped secure both political and economic advantages.

Fig 147: Former Adil shah palace
By António Lopes Mendes, India Portuguesa, 1886.

Goa: The Coastal Jewel of the Adil Shahis

The primary capital of the Adil Shahi dynasty was firmly established in Bijapur, which served as the central seat of political, administrative and cultural life.

In contrast, Goa functioned as a secondary, yet highly significant region within the Adil Shahi domain. It served primarily as a leisure retreat and strategic trading hub. Renowned for their appreciation of natural beauty, the Adil Shahs were drawn to Goa's scenic landscapes, lush greenery and coastal charm, making it an ideal setting for relaxation and royal leisure.

The presence of gardens, pleasure parks and palatial residences, such as the Adil Shah Palaces (the Old Secretariat building in Panjim and the former palace in Old Goa, of which only the gateway survives), reflects Goa's role as a favoured retreat for royalty and nobility. At the same time, Goa's strategic position along key maritime trade routes elevated its commercial importance. Its thriving ports supported the flow of horses, textiles, spices and other valuable goods, linking the Adil Shahi kingdom to broader Indian Ocean and Persian Gulf trade networks. This vibrant trade significantly enhanced Goa's status within the kingdom.

Across their kingdom, the sultans commissioned architectural monuments, cultivated a vibrant courtly culture and encouraged creative and intellectual pursuits.

Historical accounts suggest that the Adil Shahs commissioned the construction of numerous mosques across Goa, reflecting the region's cultural and religious significance during their rule. However, with the passage of time and successive waves of change, few of these structures have survived, leaving behind only traces of a once flourishing Islamic presence.

Fig 148: Adil shah Palace Gate entrance, Old Goa
Photo by Vikas Singh, CC BY-SA 4.0

The basalt stone gateway that was once the grand entrance to the Adil Shah Palace, is all that remains today, standing near St. Cajetan Church in Old Goa.

The Adil Shahi Dynasty in Goa: A Celebration of Cultural Harmony and Heritage.

The Adil Shahi dynasty is an important part of Goa's culture and history. Their influence is still visible today, in our architecture, our traditions and the values we continue to live by. Goans are known for being susegad (peaceful and content) and for embracing people of different faiths and backgrounds. This spirit of tolerance and openness has deep roots, shaped by centuries of cultural exchange.

The Adil Shahs were known for respecting all religions and cultures, a quality still evident in Goan society today. We live harmoniously in a shared garden, though our flowers may bloom in different colours of religion, caste and creed. This is clearly reflected in the structures the Adil Shahs left behind, both in Bijapur and in Goa.

Their architecture combines Persian, Indian, and local Goan elements, and often includes features inspired by both Islamic and Hindu traditions. Mosques like Safa Masjid show this beautifully, with Persian-inspired ogee arches, Portuguese/Goan-influenced pilasters and decorative elements reminiscent of Bijapur's mosques. This harmonious mix of influences showcases the Adil Shahs ability to integrate architectural elements from different traditions into a single, cohesive structure.

There was a significant connection between Persia and Bijapur, driven by shared political, social and religious views. Many scholars, merchants and Sufi sheikhs of Persian origin resided in Bijapur. These communities also took root in Goa, being an important trading hub during the Adil Shah period. The surviving dargahs attest to their presence.

From Yusuf Adil Shah, who welcomed diversity, to Ibrahim Adil Shah II, who promoted music, art and cultural harmony, the dynasty played a part in shaping the region's identity. Goa's culture today is not defined by a single influence, but by the coming together of many, and the Adil Shahs were contributors to that blend.

Although their reign was challenged by the Portuguese conquest in 1510, the Adil Shahs ruled parts of Goa that lasted over 150 years, leaving a lasting impression on its landscape and way of life. For example, the administrative framework of talukas in Goa, which is still in use today, has its roots in the systems established during the Adil Shahi period.

By remembering and protecting their legacy, we are not only preserving history but also protecting the spirit of unity and diversity that defines Goans.

The mosques and monuments of the Adil Shahs must be both preserved and celebrated in Goa, raising awareness of this rich heritage and ensuring its protection.

Fig 150: Looking onto Safa Masjid, Goa

Fig 151: Khandepar Mosque, Ponda, Goa
Photo by Salim Mulla

The Last Arches of Khandepar: A Call for Preservation

In Khandepar, lie the remains of an old mosque, of which only the impressive laterite masonry arches survive today. These arches, built in the distinctive Persian ogee style, are very similar to those found at Safa Masjid and the water tank at Surla Masjid. These surviving arches serve as a reminder of the mosque's former presence and significance in the region.

According to a formal letter submitted by Salim Mulla, a local resident and heritage advocate, to the Directorate of Archives and Archaeology, Government of Goa, the Khandepar mosque once featured a water tank and a burial ground. He attributes the loss of the tank and burial site to road construction carried out by the Public Works Department.[75] While traces of the burial ground are still visible, the tank no longer exists and has not been archaeologically documented. The letter was submitted as a formal request to conserve the site and protect it from further deterioration. However, despite many efforts, no concrete steps have been taken by the authorities to document, preserve or officially acknowledge the site.

These monuments have survived for centuries. They are not just physical structures, but historical records that reflect the culture, beliefs and artistic skills of the people who built them. Preserving them is essential, not only for historical research, but also for future generations to understand their cultural roots.

The Khandepar mosque is a valuable example of Goa's Islamic architectural heritage. Its arches are among the last visible traces of the Adil Shahi legacy in the region. They carry the story of our past, of the people, the place, and the traditions that shaped us. Today, they stand in a fragile state, slowly deteriorating due to lack of care and conservation. The architecture and craftsmanship of these structures cannot be easily replicated, even with modern technology. If we lose them, we lose a vital part of our history.

It is imperative that the Archaeological Department of Goa recognizes its significance and includes it in its conservation list before what little remains is lost forever.

Fig 152: The Neglected State of the Khandepar mosque, Ponda, Goa
Photo by Salim Mulla

The Khandepar mosque stands in a state of neglect. Preserving such heritage structures is our responsibility. Not allowing them to fall into ruin is a mark of respect for our history and cultural identity of our land.

Protecting the mosque at Khandepar is not just about preserving ruins, it is about acknowledging our past, respecting our heritage and ensuring that important cultural landmarks are not forgotten.

Note: The approximate coordinates of the Khandepar mosque are provided in Endnote 76.

Fig 153: Ruins of the, Khandepar Mosque, Ponda, Goa.
Photo by Salim Mulla

Endnotes:

1. Dr. B. Savitha, "Political and Economic Aspects of the Kadamba Empire: A Historical Analysis," International Journal of Research and Analytical Reviews (IJRAR) 10, no. 1 (2023)

2. Archaeological Committee for Goa, Daman, and Diu, Reports of the Archaeological Committee for Goa, Daman, and Diu (Goa: Government of Goa, Daman, and Diu, n.d.).

3. Maurice Hall, Window on Goa: A History and Guide (UNKNO 1992).

4. Prajal Sakhardande, Muslim History and Heritage of Goa (Mapusa: Konkani Shanti Publications, 2012), 82.

4a. Prajal Sakhardande, Goa Gold, Goa Silver: Her History, Her Heritage from Earliest Times to 2019 (Panaji: Broadway Publishing House, 2019), 73.

5. M. A. Nayeem, "External Relations of the Bijapur Kingdom (1489–1686 A.D.)" (PhD diss., University of Poona, 1973), 426

6. Nayeem, External Relations of the Bijapur Kingdom, 414

7. H. M. Stephens, Albuquerque (Oxford: Clarendon Press, 1897), 90

8. A. K. Priolkar, The Goa Inquisition (Bombay: Bombay University Press, 1961)

9. Stephens, Albuquerque, 82.

10. Afonso de Albuquerque, The Commentaries of the Great Afonso Dalboquerque, Second Viceroy of India, trans. and ed. W. de G. Birch, vol. 3 (London: Hakluyt Society, 1875), 20

11. Nayeem, External Relations of the Bijapur Kingdom, 409-452

12. Donald F. Lach and Edwin J. Van Kley, Asia in the Making of Europe, vol. 3, book 2 (Chicago: University of Chicago Press, 1993)

13. Nayeem, External Relations of the Bijapur Kingdom, 409-452

14. Jadunath Sarkar, Shivaji and His Times, 2nd ed. (London: Longmans, Green, 1920), 246.

15. Nayeem, External Relations of the Bijapur Kingdom, 391

16. Prajal Sakhardande, Goa Gold Goa Silver: Her History, Her Heritage from Earliest Times to 2019 (Panaji: Broadway Publishing House, 2019), 118

17. Seyed Salman Safavi, The Practice of Sufism and the Safavid Order (London: London Academy of Iranian Studies, 2018), chap. 2, 67.

Endnotes:

18. F. Kordi, "A Glance at the Design and Execution of Charbagh in Safavid Iran and Mughal India," Iranian Studies 4, no. 2 (2018): 49–64.

19. P. Beaumont, "The Qanat: A Means of Water Provision," in Water and Development in the Middle East, ed. T. Allan and J. Court (London: Routledge, 1996), 13–23; The Archaeologist, "The Ingenious Water Systems of Ancient Persia," The Archaeologist, February 14, 2025, https://www.thearchaeologist.org/blog/the-ingenious-water-systems-of-ancient-persia.

20. Scott C. Levi, "India xiii. Indo-Iranian Commercial Relations," Encyclopaedia Iranica, vol. XIII, fasc. 1 (2004): 44–47, last updated July 8, 2016, https://iranicaonline.org/articles/india-xiii-indo-iranian-commercial-relations.
 Willem Floor, "Commerce vi. In the Safavid and Qajar Periods," Encyclopaedia Iranica, vol. VI, fasc. 1 (1992): 67–75, last updated June 29, 2015, https://iranicaonline.org/articles/commerce-vi.

21. Elizabeth Schotten Merklinger, Indian Islamic Architecture: The Deccan 1347–1686 (Warminster, UK: Aris & Phillips Ltd, 1981)

22. Martin Frishman and Hasan-Uddin Khan, The Mosque: History, Architectural Development & Regional Diversity (London: Thames & Hudson, 1994)

23. George Michell and Mark Zebrowski, Architecture and Art of the Deccan Sultanates, vol. I, part 7 of The New Cambridge History of India (Cambridge: Cambridge University Press, 1999), 12

24. Goa, I. Decoding "The Sabaio": Sultan Yusuf Adil Shah of Bijapur. Accessed April 12, 2025. https://www.academia.edu/10046367/Decoding_The_Sabaio_Sultan_Yusuf_Adil_Shah_of_Bijapur.

25. H. Cousens, Bijapur, the Old Capital of the Adil Shahi Kings: A Guide to Its Ruins with Historical Outline (Bijapur: The Orphanage Press, 1889), 89

26. Michell and Zebrowski, Architecture and Art of the Deccan Sultanates, 13.

27. Cousens, Bijapur, the Old Capital of the Adil Shahi Kings, 94.

28. Ibid., 99.

29. Navina Najat Haidar and Marika Sardar, eds., Sultans of Deccan India, 1500–1700: Opulence and Fantasy (New York: The Metropolitan Museum of Art, 2015), 84.

30. Ibid., 6.

31. Ibid., 88

32. Ibid., 154.

Endnotes:

33. Ibid., 117.

34. Ibid., 79.

35. Donald F. Lach and Edwin J. Van Kley, Asia in the Making of Europe, vol. 3, book 2 (Chicago: University of Chicago Press, 1993), 855.

36. Haidar and Sardar, Sultans of Deccan India, 139.

37. Lach and Van Kley, Asia in the Making of Europe, 840-855.

38. Information provided verbally to the author by officials of the Archaeological Survey of India (ASI), Dharwad Circle, 2009

39. Haidar and Sardar, Sultans of Deccan India, 80.

40. Nayeem, External Relations of the Bijapur Kingdom, 62.

41. Ibid., 127.

42. Umar Khalidi, "The Shi☐ites of the Deccan: An Introduction," Rivista degli Studi Orientali 64, no. 1/2 (1990): 6.

43. Seyed Mohammad Hadi Torabi, "Safavid Dynasty Relations with Shiite Governments in India," Global Journal of Arts, Humanities and Social Sciences 7, no. 9 (October 2019) 20.

44. Nayeem, External Relations of the Bijapur Kingdom, 119.

45. Henry Heras, "Three Catholic Priests at the Court of Ali Adil Shah I," Journal of the Bombay Historical Society 1, no. 2 (1928): 158.

46. Nayeem, External Relations of the Bijapur Kingdom, 458.

47. Ibid., 458.

48. Lach and Van Kley, Asia in the Making of Europe, 846.

49. Information provided verbally to the author by officials of the Archaeological Survey of India (ASI), Dharwad Circle, 2009.

50. Richard M. Eaton, Sufis of Bijapur, 1300–1700: Social Roles of Sufis in Medieval India (New Delhi: Oxford University Press, 2000).

51. Haidar and Sardar, Sultans of Deccan India, 109.

Endnotes:

52. John Benson, Kamran Maleki, and Hadi Ghelichkhani, "Khalilullah 'Padishah of the Pen': Royal Scribe and Ambassador of Shah 'Abbas and Ibrahim 'Adil Shah II," in Iran and the Deccan: Persianate Art, Culture, and Talent in Circulation, ed. Keelan Overton (Bloomington: Indiana University Press, 2020), 367–399.

53. Paul Lunde, "The Coming of the Portuguese," Saudi Aramco World 56, no. 4 (July/August 2005): 54–61, https://archive.aramcoworld.com/issue/200504/the.coming.of.the.portuguese.htm.

54. In Goa, Asia's First Gunpowder Factory Being Razed," History News Network, published May 7, 2007, accessed April 3, 2025, https://www.historynewsnetwork.org/article/in-goa-asias-first-gunpowder-factory-being-razed.

55. R. S. Whiteway, The Rise of Portuguese Power in India, 1497–1550 (London: Susil Gupta, 1967), 224.

56. Nayeem, External Relations of the Bijapur Kingdom, 45.

57. M. N. Pearson, The Portuguese in India (Cambridge: Cambridge University Press, 1987), 54.

58. Ibid., 25-26

59. C. R. Boxer, Fidalgos in the Far East, 1550–1770: Fact and Fancy in the History of the Portuguese in Asia (London: Oxford University Press, 1968), chap. 3, "Christians and Spices: The Portuguese Padroado.

60. Lach and Van Kley, Asia in the Making of Europe, 840-855. 934-942

61. Arun Saldanha, "The Itineraries of Geography: Jan Huygen van Linschoten's 'Itinerario' and Dutch Expeditions to the Indian Ocean, 1594–1602," Annals of the Association of American Geographers 101, no. 1 (2011): 149–77, http://www.jstor.org/stable/27980165.

62. Archaeological Survey of India, Dharwad Circle, "Monuments in Vijayapura," accessed May 5, 2025, https://www.asidharwadcircle.in/monument-region/vijayapura/#s=1.

63. Maruti T. Kamble, "Adil Shahi Mosques in Karnataka," International Journal of Social Sciences and Humanity Studies 4, no. 1 (2012): 239–248, https://www.sobiad.org/eJOURNALS/journal_IJSS/arhieves/2012_1/maruti_kamble.pdf.

64. Frishman and Khan, The Mosque, 179.

65. Merklinger, Indian Islamic Architecture, 118.

66. Ibid., 118.

67. Cousens, Bijapur, the Old Capital of the Adil Shahi Kings, 97

68. M. A. Nayeem, Heritage of the Adil Shahis of Bijapur (Hyderabad: Hyderabad Publishers, 2008), 381.

Endnotes:

69. Michell and Zebrowski, Architecture and Art of the Deccan Sultanates, 88.

70. Information provided verbally to the author by officials of the Archaeological Survey of India (ASI), Goa Circle, December 2024.

71. Times of India, "Goa: Part of ASI maintained Safa Masjid collapses due to rain," July 23, 2021, http://timesofindia.indiatimes.com/articleshow/84661500.cms ;
Herald Goa, "Highway Vibrations: Cracks Show Up on Safa Masjid Walls," February 27, 2024, https://www.heraldgoa.in/Goa/Highway-vibrations-Cracks-show-up-on-Safa-Masjid-walls/218285.

71a. Times of India , "Highway Drainage Flaws Flood Ponda's Safa Masjid,", July 7, 2025, 'Highway drainage flaws flood Pondas Safa Masjid | Goa News - Times of India

72. MD Gous Choudhari, "Ancient Well of Ibrahimpur: Ibrahimpur Boudi, Bijapur, Karnataka" History Info, YouTube video, 10:42, posted April 27, 2023, https://www.youtube.com/watch?v=rgAfWLIE3ZM.

73. MD Gous Choudhari, "Masa Bauri, Masa Bawin Bijapur Karnataka," History Info, YouTube video, 9:31, December 6, 2022, https://www.youtube.com/watch?v=5IgMTNI6nDE.

74. Pilar Seminary Museum, "Adil Shahi of Bijapur," Pilar Museum, accessed March 25, 2025, https://pilarmuseum.org/adil-shahi-of-bijapur/.

75. Salim Mulla, President of the Goan Alliance Party, letter to the Directorate of Archives and Archaeology, Government of Goa, September 22, 2017. Copy in possession of the author.

76. The approximate location pin of Khandepar mosque : 15°25'29.2"N 74°02'41.5"E
The site is situated behind the VPK Urban Co-operative Society in Khandepar, Goa.

Bibliography:

- Savitha, B. "Political and Economic Aspects of the Kadamba Empire: A Historical Analysis." International Journal of Research and Analytical Reviews (IJRAR) 10, no. 1 (2023).

- Archaeological Committee for Goa, Daman, and Diu. Reports of the Archaeological Committee for Goa, Daman, and Diu. Goa: Government of Goa, Daman, and Diu, n.d.

- Wink, André. Al-Hind: The Making of the Indo-Islamic World. Vol. 1. Leiden ; New York : E.J. Brill, 1991

- Rizvi, S. A. A. The Wonder That Was India: Volume II. London: Macmillan, 1987.

- Hall, Maurice. Window on Goa: A History and Guide. UNKNO, 1992.

- Sakhardande, Prajal. Goa Gold, Goa Silver: Her History, Her Heritage from Earliest Times to 2019. Panaji: Broadway Publishing House, 2019.

- Nayeem, M. A. "External Relations of the Bijapur Kingdom (1489–1686 A.D.)." PhD diss., University of Poona, 1973.

- Stephens, H. M. Albuquerque. Oxford: Clarendon Press, 1897.

- Priolkar, A. K. The Goa Inquisition. Bombay: Bombay University Press, 1961.

- Albuquerque, Afonso de. The Commentaries of the Great Afonso Dalboquerque, Second Viceroy of India. Translated and edited by W. de G. Birch. Vol. 3. London: Hakluyt Society, 1875.

- Lach, Donald F., and Edwin J. Van Kley. Asia in the Making of Europe. Vol. 3, Book 2. Chicago: University of Chicago Press, 1993.

- Shokoohy, Mehrdad. "The Safā Masjid at Ponda, Goa — An Architectural Hybrid." South Asian Studies 13, no. 1 (1997): 71–85. https://doi.org/10.1080/02666030.1997.9628527

- Stouhi, Dima. "The Mosque Between the Past, Present, and Its Function Beyond a Religious Space." ArchDaily, April 12, 2023. https://www.archdaily.com/999537/the-mosque-between-the-past-present-and-its-function-beyond-a-religious-space.

- The Metropolitan Museum of Art. "The Mosque." The Met. Accessed March 29, 2025. https://www.metmuseum.org/learn/educators/curriculum-resources/art-of-the-islamic-world/unit-one/the-mosque-.

- Keçeci, Kagan. "The Role of Domes in Islamic Architecture." Dok Mimarlık. January 5, 2025. https://dokmimarlik.com/en/the-role-of-domes-in-islamic-architecture/

- Michell, George, and Mark Zebrowski. Architecture and Art of the Deccan Sultanates. The New Cambridge History of India I:7. Cambridge: Cambridge University Press, 1999.

Bibliography:

- Newman, A. J. The Safavid Empire. Harlow, England: Pearson Education, 2006.

- Roemer, H. R. "The Safavid Period." In The Cambridge History of Iran, Volume 6: The Timurid and Safavid Periods, edited by Peter Jackson and Laurence Lockhart. Cambridge: Cambridge University Press, 1986.

- Emami, Fatemeh. Religious Architecture of Safavid Iran. 2021. Academia. https://www.academia.edu/68882493/Religious_Architecture_of_Safavid_Iran.

- Kiani, Mohammad Yousef, and Wolfram Kleiss. Iranian Caravanserais. Tehran: Iranian Cultural Foundation, 1983.

- Architecture under Bahmanis Bijapur. Indianetzone. Accessed April 12, 2025. https://www.indianetzone.com/architecture_under_bahmanis_bijapur.

- Firishtah, History of Dekkan, trans. Jonathan Scott, vol. 1 (Shrewsbury: J. and W. Eddowes, 1794).

- Goa, I. Decoding "The Sabaio": Sultan Yusuf Adil Shah of Bijapur. Accessed April 12, 2025. https://www.academia.edu/10046367/Decoding_The_Sabaio_Sultan_Yusuf_Adil_Shah_of_Bijapur.

- Hollister, J. N. The Shi'a of India. London: Luzac and Company, 1953.

- Danvers, F. C. The Portuguese in India. Vols. 1–2. London: W. H. Allen & Co., 1894.

- Torabi, Seyed Mohammad Hadi. "Safavid Dynasty Relations with Shiite Governments in India." Global Journal of Arts, Humanities and Social Sciences 7, no. 9 (October 2019): 16–25.

- Khalidi, Umar. "The Shiʿites of the Deccan: An Introduction." Rivista degli Studi Orientali 64, no. 1/2 (1990): 5–16.

- Holt, P. M., Ann K. S. Lambton, and Bernard Lewis, eds. The Cambridge History of Islam, Volume 2: The Indian Subcontinent. Cambridge: Cambridge University Press, 1970.

- Cole, Juan R. I. Roots of North Indian Shi'ism in Iran and Iraq: Religion and State in Awadh, 1722–1859. Berkeley: University of California Press, 1988. http://ark.cdlib.org/ark:/13030/ft0f59n6r9/.

- Heras, Henry. "Three Catholic Priests at the Court of Ali Adil Shah I." Journal of the Bombay Historical Society 1, no. 2 (1928)

- Eaton, Richard M. Sufis of Bijapur, 1300–1700: Social Roles of Sufis in Medieval India. New Delhi: Oxford University Press, 2000.

- Benson, John, Kamran Maleki, and Hadi Ghelichkhani. "Khalilullah 'Padishah of the Pen': Royal Scribe and Ambassador of Shah 'Abbas and Ibrahim 'Adil Shah II." In Iran and the Deccan: Persianate Art, Culture, and Talent in Circulation, edited by Keelan Overton, 367–399. Bloomington: Indiana University Press, 2020.

Bibliography:

- Whiteway, R. S. The Rise of Portuguese Power in India, 1497–1550. London: Susil Gupta, 1967.

- Lunde, Paul. "The Coming of the Portuguese." Saudi Aramco World 56, no. 4 (July/August 2005): 54–61. https://archive.aramcoworld.com/issue/200504/the.coming.of.the.portuguese.htm.

- Subrahmanyam, Sanjay. The Portuguese Empire in Asia, 1500–1700: A Political and Economic History. 2nd ed. Chichester, UK: Wiley-Blackwell, 2012.

- Pearson, M. N. The Portuguese in India. Cambridge: Cambridge University Press, 1987.

- In Goa, Asia's First Gunpowder Factory Being Razed." History News Network. Published May 7, 2007. Accessed April 3, 2025. https://www.historynewsnetwork.org/article/in-goa-asias-first-gunpowder-factory-being-razed.

- Whiteway, R. S. The Rise of Portuguese Power in India, 1497–1550. London: Susil Gupta, 1967.

- Saldanha, Arun. "The Itineraries of Geography: Jan Huygen van Linschoten's 'Itinerario' and Dutch Expeditions to the Indian Ocean, 1594–1602." Annals of the Association of American Geographers 101, no. 1 (2011): 149–77. http://www.jstor.org/stable/27980165.

- Kamble, Maruti T. "Adil Shahi Mosques in Karnataka." International Journal of Social Sciences and Humanity Studies 4, no. 1 (2012): 239–248. https://www.sobiad.org/eJOURNALS/journal_IJSS/arhieves/2012_1/maruti_kamble.pdf.

- Nayeem, M. A. Heritage of the Adil Shahis of Bijapur. Hyderabad: Hyderabad Publishers, 2008.

- Herald Goa. "Highway Vibrations: Cracks Show up on Safa Masjid Walls." February 27, 2024. https://www.heraldgoa.in/Goa/Highway-vibrations-Cracks-show-up-on-Safa-Masjid-walls/218285.

- Times of India. "Goa: Part of ASI maintained Safa Masjid collapses due to rain" July 23, 2021. http://timesofindia.indiatimes.com/articleshow/84661500.cms.

- Levi, Scott C. "India xiii. Indo-Iranian Commercial Relations." Encyclopaedia Iranica, vol. XIII, fasc. 1 (2004): 44–47. Last updated July 8, 2016. https://iranicaonline.org/articles/india-xiii-indo-iranian-commercial-relations.

- Floor, Willem. "Commerce vi. In the Safavid and Qajar Periods." Encyclopaedia Iranica, vol. VI, fasc. 1 (1992): 67–75. Last updated June 29, 2015. https://iranicaonline.org/articles/commerce-vi.

- Pilar Seminary Museum. "Adil Shahi of Bijapur." Pilar Museum. Accessed July 25, 2025. https://pilarmuseum.org/adil-shahi-of-bijapur/.

- Sarkar, Jadunath. Shivaji and His Times. 2nd ed. London: Longmans, Green, 1920.

- Sakhardande, Prajal. Muslim History and Heritage of Goa. Mapusa: Konkani Shanti Publications, 2012.

About the Author

Tinusha Pereira is an architect with a passion for heritage, history and storytelling through design. She completed her architectural thesis in 2009, which laid the foundation for this book. Her curiosity about Goa's rich and diverse religious heritage, particularly its often-overlooked Islamic architecture, led her on a journey of discovery, from the Safa Masjid in Ponda to the historic Adil Shahi mosques in Bijapur.

Born and raised in Goa and now based in Melbourne, Tinusha blends her academic training with a deep personal connection to her cultural roots. Her work brings together measured drawings, historical research and cultural interpretation, with the hope of preserving architectural stories that are at risk of being forgotten.

She believes architecture is not just about buildings, but about people, memory and meaning. Meticulous by nature, she is driven by a desire to honour the past with both accuracy and empathy. She is also a proud mother of three, and when she is not immersed in research or design, she enjoys spending time with her family, travelling, dancing and reading.

www.ingramcontent.com/pod-product-compliance
Lightning Source LLC
Chambersburg PA
CBHW041102070526
44583CB00002B/30